29314

Editorial Adviser: N Hil

B. Sc. (Eng), C. Eng, F.I.E.

D1078206

Gorseinon College

Learning Resource Centre

Belgrave Road : Gorseinon : Swansea : SA4 6RD   Tel: (01792) 890731
This book is **YOUR RESPONSIBILITY** and is due for return/renewal
on or before the last date shown.

29314

RETURN OR RENEW - DON'T PAY FINES

Wendens Ambo, Essex

Published by E·P·A Press, Wendens Ambo, UK

The author and the publishers are grateful to the Controller, HMSO for permission to reproduce the Electricity at Work Regulations, 1989.

Additional copies of this book should be available through any good bookshop. In case of difficulty please contact the publishers directly at:

E·P·A Press
Bulse Grange
Wendens Ambo
Saffron Walden
Essex CB11 4JT

Telephone 01799 541207 Fax 01799 541166

British Library Cataloguing in Publication Data
Whitfield, J.F.
    The Guide to Electrical Safety at Work
    I. Title
    621.3

    ISBN 0 9517362 8 0 (3rd Edition)
    ISBN 0 9517362 5 6 (2nd Edition)
    ISBN 0 9517362 2 1 (1st Edition)

Printed in England by St Edmundsbury Press

Contents

Preface

The Electricity at Work Regulations 1989 came into force in Great Britain on April 1st, 1990 and in Northern Ireland on January 1st, 1992. Some months ago I became aware of the need for a publication which would present the requirements of these very important Regulations to all who need to know about them. Such people are all those who use electricity in their work — in fact, everyone who works.

Of course, all these people can obtain and read the original Regulations for themselves. They are easily obtained from Her Majesty's Stationery Office. The problem is that they are written in a form which is not easy to understand, and even more difficult to interpret. Additionally, they then refer to other publications, such as the IEE Wiring Regulations (BS 7671), British Standards, Health and Safety Executive publications, and so on. By the time all of these diverse publications had been obtained, not only would a great deal of money have been expended, but the reader would be faced with an enormous task to understand them.

It is hoped that this book will answer the questions likely to arise for people at work who need to know about, and to follow the Electricity at Work Regulations. The employed person will find what he needs to know, and the employer, as well as the self-employed, will have to hand a useful reference. The intention has been to present the material in as non-technical a manner as possible, so that it will be helpful to all. However, care has been taken to verify the accuracy of the material, so that the technical person will also find it reliable.

John Whitfield, Norwich, June, 1992

Preface to the Second Edition

When this book was written there was little experience of the applications of the new Electricity at Work Regulations. Such experience is now being gained, and has led to the expansion and revision of some of the text, notably Chapter 8 which is concerned with portable appliances. The opportunity has been taken to rewrite this Chapter, and to make adjustments and additions to the rest of the text with the intention of making the book more useful.

John Whitfield, Norwich, September, 1993

Preface to the Revised Third Edition

It is now eight years since the third edition was published, and although the vast majority of the content remains unchanged, the opportunity has been taken to update it.

A number of sections have been rewritten to reflect changes that have taken place, including publication in 2002 of BS EN 50106 which resulted in changes to the PAT code. Work has also been included on the Quality Mark Scheme for electrical contractors, voltage levels in the United Kingdom, discrimination between residual current devices, RCD types and portable appliance testers.

John Whitfield, Norwich, January 2003

Acknowledgements

The author is indebted to the following for their help during the preparation of this Guide to the Electricity at Work Regulations 1989.

Dr Katie Petty-Saphon, the Publisher, for her continued help and encouragement.

Mr N Hiller, the Editor, for his support and guidance.

Mr L Hanner, for his help in the preparation of drawings.

Mr M Bromley, of City College, Norwich, for supplying data.

Her Majesty's Stationery Office, for permission to reproduce part of the Electricity at Work Regulations 1989.

The Health and Safety Executive, for helpful advice and the provision of information.

The British Standards Institute, The Institution of Electrical Engineers, The Institution of Electronics and Electrical Incorporated Engineers, The Electrical Contractors Association, The National Inspection Council for Electrical Installation Contracting, The Amalgamated Engineers and Electrical Union, The Joint Industry Board for Electrical Contracting, for help with information concerning themselves.

His wife, for her continued forbearance and help.

Introduction

BACKGROUND

The Electricity at Work Regulations 1989 became effective in Great Britain on April 1st, 1990 and in Northern Ireland on January 1st, 1992. Their purpose is to ensure that precautions are taken against the risk of death or of personal injury from electricity in work activities. They are statutory Regulations made under the Health and Safety at Work *etc* Act 1974, intended to protect people from the dangers of electricity whilst they are at work. They replace the Electricity (Factories Act) Special Regulations of 1908 and 1944, but have a much wider scope, covering every person who is at work. The old Acts were only applicable to people working in factories, so they did not apply to hospitals, offices, educational establishments, and so on. This has now changed.

What exactly must be done to comply with these Regulations? The full answer to the question is somewhat complicated, although a full study of this book should reveal most of the answers. In simple terms, electrical systems must be safe for those using them. Electrical installations must comply with the Regulations for Electrical Installations (BS 7671), as published by the Institution of Electrical Engineers (the IEE). Appliances must be safe to use and must be regularly inspected and tested to ensure that they remain safe.

It has been said that houses are the only buildings to which the Regulations do not apply: however, anyone at work in a house, for example installing the electrical installation, extending or repairing it, or repairing or servicing electrical appliances, is at work and is thus subject to the Regulations. The new Regulations cover everyone who is at work, and it has been estimated that some sixteen million extra people in the United Kingdom are now subject to this legislation.

The Regulations apply to all electrical systems and equipment which is used in the work situation. This does not mean that any electrical installation or piece of equipment which was put into use before the Regulations became law will need automatically to be replaced. Only when the system concerned becomes unsafe must it be replaced. For example, there are still many electrical installations in constant use which were designed and installed to the 14th Edition of the IEE Wiring Regulations (which were then called 'Regulations for the Electrical Equipment of Buildings'). Provided that these installations are safe to use and do not constitute a hazard, they can continue in use. This is not to say that some modification will not be needed. If, for example, the installation includes one or more fault-voltage-operated circuit breaker, (often called voltage earth-leakage trips) these items will need to be replaced by residual current devices (sometimes called current earth-leakage trips) after a full assessment of the installation by a competent electrician.

Electrical safety is a complicated matter best left to the experts. To make an electrical system work often needs little knowledge, but to ensure safety will require a much higher level of knowledge, experience and competence.

ORGANISATIONS CONCERNED

A number of organisations is concerned with the Electricity at Work Regulations 1989, and there follow some notes on the activities, aims and constitutions of these organisations which may be helpful to the reader.

The Health and Safety Commission (HSC) and
The Health and Safety Executive (HSE)

The Commission was set up under the Health and Safety at Work *etc* Act 1974 and is responsible to the Secretary of State for Employment. Its aims are:

1. to take steps to secure the health, safety and welfare of people at work,
2. to protect the public against risks to health and safety arising out of work,
3. to conduct and to sponsor health, safety and welfare research,
4. to promote health, safety and welfare training,
5. to provide an information and advisory service.

The Commission has a Chairman and nine Commissioners who are appointed by the Secretary of State for Employment and are drawn from industry, the trade unions, local authorities and consumer interests. Most of the power of the Commission is delegated to the Health and Safety Executive, which is headed by three executive members, including a Director General and his Deputy.

The Executive employs a professional staff of factory and specialist inspectors. The organisation is arranged in seven Field Operations Divisions covering England, Wales and Scotland, as well as having twenty area offices and many more local inspectors' offices.

As a result of their findings, inspectors may issue improvement or prohibition notices. An improvement notice requires that specified remedial action is taken within a given time, whilst a prohibition notice requires a given activity to stop at once and not to resume until specified remedial steps have been taken.

The British Standards Institute (BSI)
In 1901 a paper was written which expressed concern at the many different screw and girder sizes in use, and this led to the setting up of the first Standards Committee in the same year. The success of the Committee in reducing the numbers of different types of steel products resulted in a Government grant in 1902, and the first use of the "Kitemark" in 1903 to indicate that

size and quality conformed to the agreed standard.

As time went by, the advantages of complying with Standards became more obvious, and the Institute expanded, until today there are more than 10,000 British Standards, a large proportion of which are harmonized throughout Europe. Standards do not apply only to products; for example BS 5750 has been introduced to help companies build quality and safety into the way they work so that they can always meet their customers' needs.

The Kitemark is a symbol placed on goods or equipment to indicate that they comply fully with the relevant British Standard.

The Safety Mark shows that the product bearing it has been tested and certified to cover specific safety requirements.

The Kitemark   *The Safety Mark*

There is no legal requirement for goods or equipment to meet British Standards other than those imposed by customers or by safety legislation such as the Electricity at Work Regulations 1989. However, ensuring compliance with the relevant British Standard is a good way of ensuring that the product is safe and will be interchangeable with alternative types.

The Institution of Electrical Engineers (IEE)

Founded in 1871 as the Society of Telegraph Engineers, the IEE has grown to become the largest body of professional Electrical and Electronic Engineers (current membership is in excess of 137,000) in the United Kingdom. The IEE sets high educational and professional standards for its members, and most corporate members of the Institution are Chartered Electrical Engineers, the highest grading for the electrical engineer.

In 1882 the Society produced the "Rules and Regulations for the Prevention of Fire Risks arising from Electric Lighting", the first wiring regulations in the world. Now in its 16th Edition, the "IEE Wiring Regulations" (BS 7671) is a design manual for safe electrical installations, is largely standardised with European regulations, and has become the "bible" of the electrical installer. The IEE Wiring Regulations have never had legal standing in Great Britain other than in Scotland, where compliance with them is written into the Building Regulations. However, they have always been accepted as the required standard, and most Electricity Supply Companies have been loth to connect installations to their supply systems which do not comply fully with the IEE Wiring Regulations (now BS 7671). Adoption of the Regulations as BS 7671 has given the required status. The NICEIC and the ECA (*see* below) also use the IEE Wiring Regulations (BS 7671) as the Standard to be met by their members.

Early in 2000 it seems likely that some legal backing will be given to the Wiring Regulations (BS 7671) by including them as part of the Building Regulations for England and Wales. Standards may also be improved if the Quality Mark scheme (*see* page 7) is instituted.

It may be that the frequent mention of the IEE Wiring Regulations (BS 7671) as the required standard in the Electricity at Work Regulations 1989 gives them some additional standing.

The Institution of Electronics and Electrical Incorporated Engineers (IEEIE)

The Institution of Electronics and Electrical Technician Engineers was originally formed with the assistance of the IEE as a qualifying body for technician engineers and engineering technicians. In 1990, following amalgamation with the Society of Electronics and Radio Technicians the word 'Technician' was changed to 'Incorporated', indicating the higher status enjoyed by members as entry requirements were increased. The Institution has about 30,000 members, who require a degree or a Higher National Diploma in electrical engineering or a similar discipline for corporate membership.

Members of this institution are often found in senior management positions concerned with electronics or electrical operations. They qualify as incorporated engineers (I. Eng. on the Engineering Council register) or as engineering technicians (Eng. Tech.) if Associate Members.

The Electrical Contractors' Association (ECA)

Founded in 1901, the Electrical Contractors' Association is the trade association for electrical contracting employers. Its 2,300 member firms, of all sizes, employ about 50,000 people, and are responsible for some 80% of the electrical installation work completed in England, Wales and Northern Ireland. The Electrical Contractors' Association of Scotland is a separate body providing similar services for Scottish electrical contractors.

Before joining the Association, applicants for membership are required to have been trading successfully for a minimum of three years, and all members' work is open to inspection to ensure compliance with the IEE Wiring Regulations (BS 7671) and other relevant standards. The ECA guarantees the work of its members for five years from completion and will ensure that work is completed to specification in the event of the insolvency of a member. The ECA are constituent members of the Joint Industry Board for the Electrical Contracting Industry (JIB) and of the National Inspection Council (NICEIC) (*see* below)

The National Inspection Council for Electrical Installation Contracting (NICEIC)

The National Inspection Council is a registered charity and was set up in 1956 to protect the users of electricity against unsafe and unsound electrical installations. Over 75 bodies are represented on the Council, including approvals and research bodies (such as the BSI), consumer interest organisations, the electricity supply industry, professional institutions, regulatory bodies, trade associations and the trade unions. The Council maintains a roll of approved contractors, who are regularly inspected (there are more than 40 inspectors) to ensure that their work complies fully with the IEE Wiring Regulations and British Standards, that they employ only competent electricians who are appropriately supervised, use only materials conforming to relevant British Standards, possess adequate test instruments and installation equipment, and hold £1M Public Liability Insurance. The initial inspection of a contractor's work is no sinecure. More than one third of applicants are either failed or have membership deferred. Regular re-inspection ensures that the initial high standards are maintained. There is no requirement for an electrical contractor to be a member of the NICEIC, but large and small customers are increasingly limiting their work to those who hold Membership.

The Amalgamated Engineering and Electrical Union (AEEU)
The Electrical Trades Union (ETU) was formed in 1889, and subsequent mergers brought in plumbing, electronics and telecommunication workers. In 1992 there was a merger with the Amalgamated Engineering Union to form the present organisation, which has considerably increased the size of the new trade union to about 730,000 members.

The Union was probably the first in the British Isles to negotiate an agreement requiring existing members to up-grade themselves technically following the publication of the 15th Edition of the IEE Regulations in 1981, because of the far-reaching changes in its requirements. Most installation electricians are members of the AEEU, which is a constituent member of the JIB (*see* below) and is responsible for setting education and training standards for electricians.

The Joint Industry Board for Electrical Contracting (JIB)
The JIB was formed in 1968, and is a partnership between the workers, represented by the AEEU, and the employers, largely represented by the ECA. Each side has sixteen members who sit on the Board under the control of an independent chairman. The Board is responsible for the technical education, training and grading of workers, industrial relations, health and health screening, and the safety and welfare of employees of constituents.

Most new entrants who seek to become electricians are registered by the JIB. To qualify they must pass technical examinations as well as satisfying an examiner in a series of practical tests. On satisfactory completion of the required work they can become qualified electricians. There is no longer an age requirement — at one time, a man became an electrician when he was twenty-one years old after a five-year apprenticeship, almost regardless of what he knew or what he could do.

THE QUALITY MARK SCHEME
This is a proposed approval scheme for contractors working in the domestic field. Those qualifying will be required to show that they will provide:
1   Technical capability
2   Skills and qualifications
3   Financial probity
4   A commitment to fair trading

5   A guarantee or warranty
6   Health and safety awareness
7   Liability insurance
8   Quality management
The Scheme is intended to rid the domestic building and installation field of
'cowboy' workers and contractors

RELATIONSHIPS BETWEEN THE INSPECTORS
We have seen that in addition to the work of Health and Safety Inspectors,
inspections are carried out by the National Inspection Council (NICEIC) and
the Electrical Contractors' Association (ECA). Additionally there are Local
Authority Inspectors, whose functions lie in the fields of health, hygiene and
Building Regulations, and who are not concerned with electrical safety. What
is the relationship between these officials?

Inspectors of the National Inspection Council and of the Electrical Contractors' Association are not empowered to issue improvement or prohibition
notices, or to report offenders for prosecution. If they find faults with an installation or with operational methods their ultimate sanction is to dismiss the
offender from membership of the organisation concerned. This is not to say
that they could not, in a blatant case of a continuing dangerous situation, alert
the Health and Safety Executive to the position. Inspectors of the Health and
Safety Executive are empowered to visit any work place at any time, if necessary without previous notice, to inspect the work going on. If they feel that
there is a danger of injury or to the health or welfare of people working in the
situation, they are empowered to require:
1.   an immediate halt to the activity concerned until the remedies they
       suggest are put into effect by the issue of a prohibition notice, or
2.   changes in working practices or alterations to plant and machinery
       within a specified period by the issue of an improvement notice.
The Health and Safety at Work Act *etc* 1974 makes it legal for any person
engaged in work to contact the Health and Safety Executive and to ask them to
investigate a safety problem. It seems unlikely that workers would take this
step without first asking the management to take remedial steps, but such action is perfectly possible.

QUALIFICATIONS AND COMPETENCE

For the employer or employee who is not directly engaged in electrical work, as well as for many who are, the range of qualifications in the electrical field is a closed book. In much of the world, the word "engineer" has a special meaning, and cannot be used by all and sundry any more than can the title "doctor". In the United Kingdom this is not so, and all of us have come across the partly skilled mechanic who describes himself as an engineer. All relevant qualifications are validated by the Engineering Council.

Perhaps the following list will go some way to clarifying the position. It is written in order of seniority. The qualifications for each level are correct at the time of writing, but individual Institutions may change their entry requirements as has happened in the past.

Chartered Engineer (C. Eng.)
To become a Chartered Engineer an applicant must have reached a stipulated age and must demonstrate suitable educational qualifications, training and experience to a high level. The educational qualification is an approved first or second class honours degree from a University validated by the Institution of Electrical Engineers, and the experience requirement is three or more years in a responsible position as an electrical engineer. Chartered Electrical Engineers will be corporate members of the IEE and may put the designatory letters for a Fellow (C. Eng., FIEE) or a Member (C. Eng., MIEE) after their names. There will be many Chartered Engineers who serve different disciplines and are Members of other Institutions, but such people will not usually be considered competent to deal with electrical matters.

Incorporated Engineer (I. Eng.)
A minimum age, a stated level of academic attainment, as well as suitable training and experience are the requirements for this qualification. Incorporated Engineers will be Fellows or Members of the Institution of Electronics and Electrical Incorporated Engineers (I. Eng., FIEIE or I. Eng., MIEIE) and will be recognised by the use of these letters after their names. The level of academic qualification required is a suitable degree or a Higher National Diploma in electrical engineering. Incorporated Engineers will typically deal with matters at a slightly lower level than Chartered Engineers, but are likely to carry considerable responsibility.

Engineering Technician (Eng. Tech.)
This qualification can be identified by the letters I. Eng., AMIEIE after the name of the person concerned. Associate Members of the IEEIE are required to have a National or Higher National Certificate in electrical engineering, as well as suitable training and experience. Engineering Technicians may well carry out complicated technical tasks, such as testing an electrical installation.

Qualified Electrician (no designatory letters)
Qualified electricians will have met the academic and practical requirements of the Joint Industry Board for the Electrical Contracting Industry (JIB). Usually electricians cannot be accepted into their trade union (AEEU) until they are suitably qualified, although there is a number of unqualified electricians who work for themselves or for non-unionised firms.

Unqualified Workers
There is a need in every organisation for unqualified people to carry out technical work under supervision, described by the IEE Wiring Regulations as "instructed persons". Such people may well carry out work such as lamp cleaning, the routine testing of portable appliances using a special test set (PAT) as described in Chapter 8, and so on, and which would otherwise require a qualified person.

Competence
The competence of a person to carry out a given task is difficult to assess. Someone qualified in one of the categories described above could be assumed to be competent to carry out work at the level of his qualification, but the problem remains of assessing competence amongst those with different qualifications and for those who have no qualifications at all.

In these cases, it is for the employer to judge the level of competence required, and to ensure that no person is called on to carry out work for which he does not have the required competence. This is very much a matter of individual judgement, but the employer or the employee must always bear in mind the fact that he may be required to justify his decisions before a court of law in the event of an accident.

There is a clear need for every organisation to have a programme of industrial training and re-training for all employees to increase or to maintain levels of competence in the interests of safety as well as of productivity.

REQUIREMENTS OF THE REGULATIONS

Employers and the self-employed must comply with the requirements of the Electricity at Work Regulations 1989 in as far as they deal with matters which are in their direct control. Employees are required to co-operate with their employers to enable them to comply with the duties placed upon them by the Regulations.

The Regulations use the terms "absolute" and "as far as is reasonably practicable" to indicate the levels of duty imposed. The terms are described in Chapter 1 of this book, and an understanding of them is essential for the employer and the employee who uses electricity at work. It must be clearly understood that a failure to comply may be a criminal offence, which can be punished with a fine and/or with a prison sentence. Such a conviction would not prevent a civil action also being brought for damages as a result of the failure to comply.

The Regulations must cover changes necessarily occurring to safety practices with time and thus are written in general terms. They are not written to provide details of the methods of compliance, but refer to British Standards, Codes of Practice, and the current Edition of the IEE Wiring Regulations (BS 7671) as the required arbiters of the levels of work required. Titles of many of these documents are listed in Appendix 2 of this book. They are consistent in stressing that work should never be carried out on live electrical systems unless it is absolutely essential to do so.

An important requirement of the Regulations is periodic inspection and testing of portable appliances used at work. In this context, a home is not considered to be a place of work, but all other appliances are subject to this requirement as indicated in Chapter 8.

For further details of applicable Standards and publications, Appendix 2 contains a useful list, complete with a separate alphabetical index. The full Electricity at Work Regulations 1989, apart from those applying only to mines and quarries, are reproduced as Appendix 1, by the kind permission of the Health and Safety Executive. This Appendix is also provided with its own alphabetical index.

1
The Legal Position

1.1 BACKGROUND TO THE REGULATIONS (Regulation 1)

The Health and Safety at Work *etc* Act was passed in 1974, and was novel for the United Kingdom in that it requires everybody who is concerned with work (both employers and employees) to be aware of their own safety and that of others. For the first time, a failure to take account of safety of people at work, whether of one's self or of others, became a criminal offence, which could be punished by a prison sentence. During its early years there was some doubt as to exactly who was covered by the Act. Did it, for example, include hospitals, establishments of learning such as schools and colleges, places of entertainment, and so on?

In recent years it has become understood that this legislation covers every person who is 'at work'. Thus, schools and colleges are covered because those teaching in them are at work, hospitals are included since medical and ancillary staff are working, and so are theatres and other places of entertainment because people (the actors, the stage staff, the managers, the ushers, *etc*.) are working. The only place not covered is the home, because here people are not working (no doubt the housewife would have something to say on this subject!). However, any person who is employed to carry out work in a home is covered and must comply with the Regulations.

The Electricity at Work Regulations 1989 were conceived by the Health and Safety Executive after wide consultation, and became law on April 1st, 1990, enabled by the Health and Safety at Work *etc* Act, 1974. They are written in four parts, which are:

Part I	Introduction	Regulations 1 to 3
Part II	General	Regulations 4 to 16

Part III   Applies to mines and quarries only
            Regulations 17 to 28 (*Note that the regulations for*
mines and quarries are not covered by this guide)
Part IV   Miscellaneous Regulations 29 to 33
All of the Regulations with the exception of those dealing specifically with mines and quarries are included here as Appendix 1 with the kind permission of the Health and Safety Executive.

1.2 MAIN CHANGES AND INTERPRETATION
1.2.1 Changes (Regulations 2, 3, 14 and 16)
Prior to the introduction of the Electricity at Work Regulations 1989 early in 1990, electrical work was governed by the Factories Acts, a prime reason for the doubt as to what situations outside factories were actually covered. The changes which follow from the introduction of the 1989 Regulations may be summed up as:

1. there is no need to display 'electric shock' notices, which were previously required to give instruction on what to do in the event of a shock. The requirement now is that all people at work must be capable of dealing with the results of such a shock, and there must be a trained body of persons immediately available for the purpose.

2. it is now the duty of every employer (or self-employed person) to comply with the requirements of the Regulations, and of every employee to co-operate with his employer to see that the Regulations are followed as far as it is in his power so to do.

3. live line working is very strongly discouraged unless it is 'unreasonable in all the circumstances' for the system concerned to be dead. Any worker or employer who tolerates working on an electrical system whilst it is live, will now have to produce a very good reason for doing so, as well as very comprehensive proof of the competence of the worker(s) to work in that situation.

4. the age limitations of the old Factories Acts, which prevented young persons from carrying out electrical work have been removed. Competence, rather than age, is now the required criterion.

5. there is no longer a distinction between high voltage and low voltage. All persons working with electrical systems, at whatever voltage, are

subject to the 1989 Regulations. This also removes the confusion existing because the IEE Wiring Regulations and the Factories Acts used different definitions of high and low voltage classifications.

6. there is now a requirement for adequate supervision of all workers who are using an electrical system. The object is to prevent risk of injury or of danger due to a lack of skills on the part of themselves or of others.

7. there are fewer definitions. This is the subject of the next section.

1.2.2 Definitions (Regulation 2)
Whilst the number of definitions has reduced, those that remain are clearly stated. They include:

Conductor
A conductor is defined as 'a conductor of electrical energy'. The definition shows that the term includes anything which can act as conductor, whether normally expected to do so or not. As well as cables intended to carry current, it includes metal structures, earth systems and so on.

Many materials which we would not, perhaps, usually classify as conductors must be included, such as salt water, ionised gases, and conducting particles. Account must be taken of the changes to conductance as a result of temperature change; we usually think of glass, for example, as an insulator. However, when it becomes molten it is a conductor, and must be considered as such when in this state.

Circuit conductor
This term is used to describe a conductor whose normal function is to carry load current or to be energised, and thus covers all cables installed for these purposes. Since a protective conductor (earth wire) will not normally be expected to carry current, and will only do so in the event of a fault, it cannot be classified as a circuit conductor although it may be or can be a conductor.

Electrical equipment
This term includes every type of device using electricity for its operation. The range varies from the 400 kV circuit breakers used by the power generation and transmission companies to a 1.5 V battery powered handlamp. Since these Regulations are concerned with safety, it is obvious why they

deal with high voltage devices, but perhaps not so clear why very low voltage devices, from which an electric shock is not possible, are included. The reason is that it is not impossible, for example, for a low power battery to provide the energy needed to initiate the explosion of a flammable gas.

System

This term includes all the parts which go to make up the complete system, including the source of supply, the equipment and the conductors. The term is not limited simply to parts in electrical contact; for example, the primary and secondary windings of a transformer are electrically separate but are connected magnetically and so are part of the same system. This means that normal electrical installations are part of an electrical system extending over a very wide geographical area due to interconnection through the supply transformers of the distribution system.

Equipment which is disconnected from a system, but which can be readily reconnected to it, must be considered to be part of that system. For example, if a circuit is separated by removal of fuses or links from a system, it must still be considered to be part of that system. In some cases, a system which is disconnected from its source of supply, and thus dead, may become live during testing. For example, an insulation resistance test on a normal circuit will usually require the application of at least 500 V to that circuit and may cause danger to people who touch the circuit during the test.

Danger

Danger is defined as 'a risk of injury'. It follows that the expression 'to prevent danger' means 'to prevent the risk of injury'. The question immediately arises as to why both terms are necessary. The position is that if people are required to work on live systems they will always be in danger whilst doing so, but injury must be prevented. If no danger arises from a particular system, no precautions need to be taken; this assumes that there is no risk of electric shock, of fire, of electric burn, of arcing or of explosion.

Injury

The purpose of the Regulations is to prevent death or personal injury from electrical causes in connection with work activities. The term 'injury' means death or injury to people due to:

1. electric shock,
2. electric burn,
3. fires of electrical origin,
4. electric arcing, or
5. explosions caused by the use of electricity.

Charged/live
Strictly these two words have different meanings, but their effects are similar as far as safety is concerned. The word 'live' means that the system is connected to a voltage as in normal use. 'Charged' means that the system is live, or that it has acquired a charge by some other means, such as static electricity, an induced voltage due to electromagnetic coupling, or a retained charge due to capacitive effects.

Dead
Any system which is 'dead' is neither live nor charged, and can be taken as posing no danger.

1.2.3 Injury hazards (Regulation 2)
The previous section listed five causes of injury. These are explained in greater detail in Chapter 2.

1.3 LEVELS OF DUTY (Regulations 3, 6, 7, 14 and 15)
1.3.1 Duties of an employer (Regulation 3)
The definition of the word 'employer' is of interest. An employer is any person who employs one or more individuals under a contract of employment or apprenticeship or who provides training under the schemes to which the Health and Safety at Work *etc*. Act applies. A self-employed person is also defined as an employer, whether or not he employs others.

Under the requirements of the Health and Safety at Work *etc*. Act 1974 it is the duty of the employer to provide, so far as is reasonably practical:

1. adequate information, supervision and instruction to ensure that work with electrical systems can be carried out safely, and
2. a safe place of work, including adequate working space, access and lighting and

3. a safe working environment, so that all electrical equipment is selected to be suitable for use in its expected surroundings including the use of equipment which has been certified to conform to the relevant standards. The equipment must be selected bearing in mind the environment in which it will perform, due attention being given to the possibilities of mechanical damage, weather and other natural hazards, corrosion, dirt and dust (including combustible dusts) possible explosive atmospheres and other flammable substances, and the prevention of ingress of water or mechanical objects (the Index of Protection (IP) system is explained in Section 4.6). Also included is the safe insulation, protection and placing of conductors, as well as cutting off electrical supplies to make the electrical system safe where this is appropriate, and

4. a safe plant, and where appropriate, safe systems of working, particularly applying to live working on electrical systems, and

5. a safe system for handling articles and substances, the systems depending on the nature of the articles or substances concerned. For example, if employees are required to handle corrosive substances in connection with the cleaning of electrical equipments, they must be provided with the necessary protective clothing and equipment.

Regulation 3 makes clear that it is the duty of every employer to comply with the requirements of the Regulations in so far as they apply to matters which are within his control.

1.3.2 Duties of an Employee (Regulation 3)
Every employee whilst at work must:

1. co-operate with his employer to enable the duty placed on that employer by the Regulations to be carried out, and

2. comply with the Regulations in so far as they relate to matters which are within his control.

Thus the duties placed on the employee are equivalent to those placed on the employer in situations which are in his direct control. In this respect, it is worth noting that trainees have exactly the same duties as other employees. The arrangement recognises that to a large extent employees engaged in electrical work often carry an unusually high level of responsibility for their actions and for safety, both of themselves and of others. The degree of 'control' that they exercise over electrical safety in a particular situation will determine the extent to which they hold responsibilities so as to ensure compliance with the Regulations.

The nature of electrical systems is such that it is perfectly possible for an employee to be responsible for danger at a point beyond his own installation. An example would be when he connects from his installation onto other parts of the system, without having proper authorisation to do so. In such a case, the employee would become entirely responsible for dangers which arose. In such a situation, he would be called the duty holder.

1.4   TYPES OF DUTY (Regulations 3 and 29)

There are two levels of duty indicated in the Regulations:

1. absolute
2. as far as is reasonably practicable.

1.4.1   Absolute Duty   (Regulation 3)

Any duty which is absolute is a requirement which must be met regardless of cost or of any other consideration. An example is Regulation 5, which requires that the strength and capability of electrical equipment must not be exceeded in such a way as may give rise to danger. For example, it is not permissible to install light duty (500 V rated) mineral insulated cables in a situation such as the starting and ignition circuit of a discharge lamp where it is known that higher voltages will be present. The cable used must be suitable for the known conditions.

The defence against a charge of failing in the requirement for absolute duty is contained in Regulation 29 and applies only to criminal (not civil) prosecutions. The defence is that the person should prove that all reasonable steps were taken and all due diligence exercised to avoid committing an offence. This defence will apply to:

Regulation 4(4)   Protective electrical equipment

Regulation 5   Strength and capability of electrical equipment

Regulation 8	Earthing or other suitable precautions
Regulation 9	Integrity of referenced conductors
Regulation 10	Connections
Regulation 11	Means for protecting from excess current
Regulation 12	Means for cutting off the supply and for isolation
Regulation 13	Precautions for work on equipment made dead
Regulation 14	Work on or near live conductors
Regulation 15	Working space, access and lighting
Regulation 16	Persons to be competent to prevent danger and injury

1.4.2 Duty so far as is reasonably practicable (Regulation 3)

There will be situations where the likelihood of an accident is considered to be remote, and where the costs of taking steps to ensure that such an occurrence of an accident is impossible in terms of physical difficulty, time, trouble and expense are unacceptably high. In such a case it might be considered that taking the necessary safety steps is not 'reasonably practicable'.

In many situations the results of an electrical accident could be very severe (for example, death from electrocution) whilst the cost of preventing it (possibly the provision of insulation) might be low. In such a case, the level of duty to prevent the danger comes close to that of an absolute duty. In the event of a prosecution following an accident, the lack of finance to effect safety would not be an acceptable defence. In the case of a person pleading a defence of having done all that was reasonably practicable, it would be for the defendant to prove that he **had** done all that was reasonably practicable.

A defence under the heading of 'so far as is reasonably practicable' would particularly apply to:

Regulation 4(1)	System construction to prevent danger
Regulation 4(2)	System maintenance to prevent danger

Regulation 4(3)   System use to prevent danger

Regulation 6   Adverse or hazardous environments

Regulation 7   Insulation, protection and placing of conductors

To sum up, an absolute duty must be met, regardless of inconvenience or cost. If the duty is so far as is reasonably practicable, all sensible steps must be taken to fulfil it.

1.5 OTHER REGULATIONS

The last four Regulations are concerned with 'tying up loose ends', and since they are concerned mainly with legalities, they are considered in this Chapter.

1.5.1 Exemption certificates (Regulation 30)
Regulation 30 allows the Health and Safety Executive to exempt from the Regulations any person, premises, electrical equipment, electrical system, electrical process, or activity. This exemption allows for the Regulations to be waived in special cases, possibly for a limited time, provided that the Executive is sure that the health and safety of persons will not be affected by it.

It is difficult to visualise a situation in which this exemption would be brought into use. A possibility is that during a war it may be considered that the safety of a whole group of people under attack is of more importance than that of a limited number who may be concerned with the defence of the majority.

1.5.2 Extension outside Great Britain (Regulation 31)
This Regulation deals with the extension of the requirements of the Regulations outside Great Britain but within its territorial waters such as oil and gas rigs. At present such situations are not subject to the Regulations.

Attention is drawn to the manufacture of equipment within Great Britain but intended for use outside. Such equipment is not subject to the Regulations, except when it is energised whilst within Great Britain for test purposes.

1.5.3 Disapplication of duties (Regulation 32)

Sea-going ships are subject to other electrical safety legislation, so the Regulations do not apply to normal ship-board activities of the ship's crew under the direction of their master. However, if a ship is brought to a port in Great Britain for service or repair, a shore-based contractor will be subject to the Regulations as long as the ship remains in territorial waters.

The Regulations only apply to aircraft and hovercraft whilst they are not moving under their own power.

1.5.4 Revocations and modifications (Regulation 33)

This Regulation indicates that the Regulations modify a number of statutory provisions, such as the Electrical Factories Acts.

1.6 PENALTIES

The Electricity at Work Regulations are made under the Health and Safety at Work Act and penalties are imposed under Section 33 of the latter. Offences are tried in the Magistrates Courts (Sheriff court without jury in Scotland) and may be sent on to the Crown Court (Sheriff court with jury in Scotland) depending on the seriousness of the case. Defendants may ask for jury trial, the decision being that of the magistrates.

Where the case is tried in the Magistrates Court the maximum penalty is £5,000 except where the offence is failure to comply with an improvement or prohibition notice, when the penalty can be imprisonment for up to 6 months or a fine of up to £20,000 or both. If, having been found guilty of failing to comply with an improvement or prohibition notice, there is a continuing failure to comply, an additional fine of £100 may apply for each day of failure.

2.1 INJURY (Regulations 2 and 16)

Two terms used in the Regulations are danger and injury. Danger is defined as "the risk of injury", so the two are closely related. It may seem that there is no point in having two terms where one would do. However, in one case [Regulation 16] the wording becomes "to prevent danger, or where appropriate, injury".

This would apply to a situation such as live working, where it may be impossible for the electrical supply to be cut off. In such a case, danger cannot be prevented, but injury certainly can.

2.2 CAUSES OF INJURY (Regulation 2)

There are five causes of injury listed in the Regulations. They are:

1. Electric shock
The subject is covered in detail in Chapter 6.

2. Electric burn
Electric burns are not the same as those due to fire, arcing or explosion. They are due to the heating effect of electric current passing through the body tissues, and thus are usually associated with electric shock, often occurring in or on the skin at the point of contact with the electrical system. In the case of radio frequency (RF) systems, the heating is by electromagnetic waves (microwaves) and direct contact with the electrical system is not necessarily required. Such burns may take place deep within the body and possibly without the sensation of electric shock.

Electric burns are usually very painful and slow to heal, and often will result in permanent scarring.

3. Fires of electrical origin
Electricity can cause fire in a number of ways, including:

1.   overheating of conductors and cables due to carrying more current than was intended (overloading),
2.   current leaking to earth or between conductors due to low levels of insulation resistance as a result of poor or inadequate insulation,
3.   overheating of flammable* materials placed too close to electrical equipment which is operating normally,
4.   ignition of flammable* materials as a result of electric arcing or of the scattering of hot particles (explosion) as a result of an electrical fault.

Injuries due to fire are usually burns, but may also be as a result of the inhalation of smoke.

* There is a very widespread misunderstanding of the term "flammable". For very many years the word "inflammable" was used to describe something which could catch fire and thus become dangerous. This word sometimes caused confusion, because the prefix "in" means "not" (for example, "indirect") so that "inflammable" was sometimes wrongly assumed to mean "not flammable". The position was clarified by outlawing the word "inflammable", although its use is still not uncommon. In its place, we use "non flammable", the word "flammable" being used to describe materials which will burn.

4. Electric arcing
An electric arc takes place when current flows through the air or through insulation between two conductors at different potentials. The path of the current becomes conducting due to the ionisation of the gas (often air), the resistance of the arc path sometimes being reduced by the presence of conductive particles removed from the conductors themselves by the heat of the arc. Since arcs are often associated with faults, the current level, and hence the heating effect, is usually great.

Injury from arcs may be as a direct result of burning from the arc, in which case it is not unusual for the severity of the burn to be increased because molten metallic conductor particles may enter the burn. Arc burns are usually very severe and are often fatal. The arc will also emit very large quantities of energy in the ultra-violet part of the electromagnetic spectrum, so that skin exposed to such radiation becomes burned in a similar way to that experienced as a result of prolonged exposure to the sun. The eyes are particularly sensitive to such radiation, and may suffer severe pain after exposure (this is the same as "arc eye" sometimes experienced by arc welders).

5. Explosion caused by the use of electricity

An explosion of any type is usually associated with the sudden release of a large quantity of energy. All sorts of electrical equipments, such as motors, switchgear and heavy power cables, may explode violently when they are subject to much higher levels of current than they are designed to carry. This could be due to the large amounts of heat energy produced, and/or to the very high electromagnetic forces involved. These forces apply to any current carrying conductor which is subject to a magnetic field. Since the current itself sets up the magnetic field, any conductor carrying current which is close to a similar conductor will be subjected to this force, which depends on the product of the two currents. Thus, if a momentary fault current is one thousand times normal in both conductors, the force during the same period will be one million times greater!

Other explosions may be caused by the ignition of flammable vapours, gases, liquids or dust due to electrical fault or to the high surface temperature of a piece of electrical equipment.

3.1 DEFINITIONS (Regulation 16)

It will be self evident that those engaged in using electricity at their work must be competent to do so. It follows that specialists concerned with the design, installation and maintenance of electrical systems must have the experience and training necessary to make them competent in what they are doing. The over-riding requirement is that those at work should not put themselves or others in danger because they lack competence in what they are doing.

This requirement of competence applies to both employees and to employers and is cited both in the Health and Safety at Work Act 1974 and in the Electricity at Work Regulations 1989.

The Regulations do not include a definition of competence. For example, they do not say that electricians are not able to install electrical systems unless they have completed an approved apprenticeship, or that school teachers may not operate film projectors without having completed a training course on the subject. Neither do the Regulations indicate an age limit. There is nothing to say, for example, that a particular machine can be operated only by workers who have reached eighteen years of age or more; neither is there any stated upper age limit.

The reader may find it useful to consult the section of the Introduction which deals with qualifications.

3.2 AN EMPLOYER'S DUTIES (Regulations 3 and 16)

It is the duty of the employer to ensure that all who install, maintain or operate electrical systems in the workplace for which responsibility is held are competent to do so. Some technical expertise will be involved to appreciate the dangers which could occur, and to know when they are not competent to judge the situation but need to take expert advice. Such advice is always available from the Health and Safety Executive. The employer has the responsibility to:

1.   provide supervision for workers if they need back-up help or advice. The need for supervision is for the employer to decide, but he must always keep in mind that he must be prepared to give reasons for the course of action taken should an accident occur,

2.   keep training records for his employees. A possible defence in the event of a breach of Regulation 16 would be to show that full and proper training had been undertaken by those involved. Training records, which should include the results of tests to verify competence, would be essential in such a case,

3.   staff whose main occupation is other than that in which they are engaged. Training must be provided and competence tested, and

4.   contractors employed for electrical work. Employing a contractor does not absolve the employer from all responsibility under Regulation 3, and there must be:
    a)   provision of full information concerning the electrical system,
    b)   provision of any other information which may affect the safety of the contractor's staff, and
    c)   a clear contract or other agreement concerning the division of safety responsibilities between the employer and the contractor.

3.3 AN EMPLOYEE'S DUTIES (Regulations 3 and 16)

Both the Health and Safety at Work Act 1974 and the Electricity at Work Regulations 1989 require that employees do not put themselves in danger as a result of their lack of competence to carry out the tasks they are attempting. It follows that all those engaged in electrical work need to:

1.   appreciate the dangers involved in the work they are undertaking,

2.   recognise when such dangers are present,

3.   understand and implement safe working practices which remove the danger, and

4.   understand the different types of injury which could occur if the working methods used are faulty or ineffective.

It follows that the employee concerned should have the technical knowledge and experience necessary to comply with the requirements above, which will include:

1.   the necessary experience of electrical work of the kind they are performing,

2.   a suitable understanding of the system on which they are working as well as practical experience of that system,

3.   a suitable knowledge of the principles of electricity

4.   an understanding of the dangers which could arise in the work being performed, and

5.   the ability to know if it is safe to continue with the work in hand.

System Design and Installation

4.1 INTRODUCTION

This chapter will be concerned with the design and installation of an electrical system which will remain safe to use during its intended lifetime. It will cover the requirements of a number of the Regulations concerned with the construction and installation of the system, including provision for its safe maintenance.

We hear a great deal these days about the importance of electromagnetic compatibility (EMC) and protecting equipments from the effects of electromagnetic radiation (EMR). It should be stressed that whilst the effects of producing such fields by switching loads and in other ways can be very serious for equipment, such as the loss of memory or the adulteration of stored data, it does not present a human injury danger and is thus not considered in this book.

4.2 INITIAL ASSESSMENT (Regulations 5 and 6)

Regulation 5 indicates that electrical equipment used in a design must be such that it will not fail in expected use and will be capable of dealing with the operational conditions. Whilst the Electricity at Work Regulations are written in general terms, compliance with the current edition of the Regulations for Electrical Installations, published by the Institution of Electrical Engineers (the IEE Wiring Regulations) (BS 7671) will always satisfy their requirements. In this connection, it may be helpful to mention "The Electrician's Guide to the 16th Edition of the IEE Wiring Regulations" by John Whitfield, published by EPA Press of Wendens Ambo, Essex, which provides helpful explanations of these important Regulations.

Regulation 5 means that the installation designer must ensure that the system and its components are capable of dealing with all possible eventualities, both normal and abnormal. To do so he must ensure that he assesses:

1. maximum demand and diversity,
2. the sizes of cables to be installed, and
3. the ratings of switches, fuses, circuit breakers *etc.*

A commonly misunderstood requirement for the safe design of an electrical installation concerns the need to select equipment which will safely handle the prospective fault current of the system. The prospective fault current (sometimes called the prospective short-circuit current, or PSC) is the highest value of current likely to flow in the part of the installation concerned in the event of a short-circuit fault, either between live conductors or to earth. Protective devices, such as fuses and circuit breakers, must then be able safely to interrupt the fault current without resulting in a failure, such as an explosion or fire.

The requirements of Regulation 6 include the need to choose systems so that there will be no danger when they are exposed to adverse conditions which reasonably could be foreseen. These conditions include those described in section 4.6.

4.3 MAXIMUM DEMAND AND DIVERSITY
4.3.1 Maximum Demand (Regulation 5)
Maximum demand (often referred to as MD) is the total current which would be carried by circuits, switches and protective devices if all loads were simultaneously connected; it does not include the levels of current flowing under overload or short circuit conditions. Assessment of maximum demand is sometimes straightforward. For example, the maximum demand of a 240 V single-phase 7 kW shower heater can be calculated by dividing the power (7 kW) by the voltage (240 V) to give a current of 29.2 A. This calculation assumes a power factor of unity, which is a reasonable assumption for such a purely resistive load.

There are times, however, when assessment of maximum demand is less obvious. For example, if a ring circuit feeds twenty 13 A sockets, the maximum demand clearly should not be 20 x 13 = 260 A, if only because the circuit protection will not be rated at more than 32 A. Some 13 A sockets may feed bench lights with 60 W lamps fitted, whilst others may feed 3 kW heaters; others again may not be loaded at all. Guidance on the assumed current demand of outlets is given in {Table 4.1}.

Table 4.1 Current demand of outlets	
Type of outlet	*Assumed current demand*
2 A socket outlet	At least 0.5 A
Other socket outlets	Rated current
Lighting point	Connected load, with minimum of 100 W
Shaver outlet, bell transformer or any equipment of 5 W or less	May be neglected
Household cooker	10 A + 30% of remainder + 5 A for socket in cooker unit

Lighting circuits pose a special problem when determining MD. Each lampholder must be assumed to carry the current required by the connected load, subject to a minimum loading of 100 W per lampholder (a demand of 0.42 A per lampholder at 240 V). Discharge lamps are particularly difficult to assess, as current cannot be calculated simply by dividing lamp power by supply voltage. The reasons for this are:

1   control gear losses result in additional current,
2   the power factor is usually less than unity so current is greater, and
3   chokes and other control gear, including fully electronic types, usually distort the waveform of the current so that it contains harmonics which are additional to the fundamental supply current.

So long as the power factor of a discharge lighting circuit is not less than 0.85, the current demand for the circuit can be calculated from:

$$\text{current (A)} \quad = \quad \frac{\text{lamp power (W)} \times 1.8}{\text{supply voltage (V)}}$$

For example, the steady state current demand of a 240 V circuit supplying eight 65 W fluorescent lamps would be:

$$I \quad = \quad \frac{8 \times 65 \times 1.8}{240} \text{ A} \quad = \quad 3.90 \text{ A}$$

Switches for circuits feeding discharge lamps must be rated at twice the steady-state current they are required to carry, unless they have been specially constructed to withstand the severe arcing resulting from the switching of such inductive and capacitive loads.

Electrical equipment must have an overall strength and capability to withstand the thermal, electromagnetic, electrochemical or other effects of the electric current which might be expected to flow. As well as normal load currents, the system may have to carry:

1.   transient overloads (overloads of short duration),
2.   fault current,
3.   pulses of current (for example, due to initial switching of a lighting system or the starting of a motor),
4.   low power factor circuits (where the current may be higher than expected), or
5.   harmonic currents, which are alternating values of current at a multiple of the basic frequency. For example, the neutral of a four-wire three-phase system may well carry high third harmonic currents (at 150 Hz), particularly where the load contains electromagnetic equipments such as transformers, discharge lighting, *etc*.

When assessing maximum demand, account must be taken of the possible growth in demand during the life of the installation. Apart from indicating that maximum demand must be assessed, the IEE Wiring Regulations (BS 7671) themselves give little help.

4.3.2 Diversity (Regulation 5)

A ring circuit in a school may feed a large number of 13 A sockets but is usually protected by a fuse or circuit breaker rated at 30 A or 32 A. This means that if sockets were feeding 13 A loads, more than two of them in use at the same time would overload the circuit and it would be disconnected by its protective device.

In practice, the chance of all ring sockets feeding loads taking 13 A is small. Whilst, in such a school, there may be a 3 kW washing machine in the domestic science room, a 3 kW heater in the staff room and another in the head teacher's room, the chance of all three being in use at the same time is unlikely provided that the installation has been correctly designed. If they are all connected at the same time, this could be seen as a failure of the designer when assessing the installation requirements; the installation should have had two or more ring circuits to feed the parts of the school in question.

Most sockets, then, will feed smaller loads such as lamps, soldering irons, video or audio machines and so on. The chances of all the sockets being used simultaneously is remote in the extreme provided that the number of sockets (and ring circuits) installed is large enough. The condition that only a few sockets will be in use at the same time, and that the loads they feed will be small is called diversity.

By making allowance for reasonable diversity, the number of circuits and their rating can be reduced, with a consequent financial saving, but without reducing the effectiveness of the installation. However, if diversity is over-estimated, the normal current demands will exceed the ratings of the protective devices, which will disconnect the circuits — not a welcome prospect for the user of the installation! Overheating may also result from overloading which exceeds the rating of the protective device, but does not reach its operating current in a reasonably short time. The IEE Wiring Regulations (BS 7671) require that circuit design should prevent the occurrence of small overloads of long duration.

The sensible application of diversity to the design of an installation calls for experience and a detailed knowledge of the intended use of the installation. Future possible increases in load should also be taken into account. Diversity relies on a number of factors which can only be properly assessed in the light of detailed knowledge of the type of installation, the industrial process concerned where this applies, and the habits and practices of the users. Perhaps a glimpse into a crystal ball to foresee the future could also be useful!

4.3.3 Applied diversity

Table 4.2 Allowance for diversity

Note the following abbreviations:
X is the full load current of the largest appliance or circuit
Y is the full load current of the second largest appliance or circuit
Z is the full load current of the remaining appliances or circuits

Type of final circuit	Types of premises	
	Small shops, stores, offices	*Hotels, guest houses*
Lighting	90% total demand	75% total demand
Heating & power	100%X + 75%(Y + Z)	100%X + 80%Y + 60%Z
Cookers	100%X + 80%Y + 60%Z	100%X + 80%Y + 60%Z
Motors (but not lifts)	100%X + 80%Y + 60%Z	100%X + 50%(Y+Z)
Instantaneous water heaters	100%X + 100%Y + 25%Z	100%X + 100%Y + 25%Z
Thermostatic water heaters	100%	100%
Floor warming installations	100%	100%
Thermal storage heating	100%	100%
Standard circuits	100%X + 50%(Y+Z)	100%X + 50%(Y+Z)
Sockets and stationary equip.	100% X + 75% (Y+Z)	100% X + 75% Y+ 40%Z

Apart from indicating that diversity and maximum demand must be assessed, the IEE Wiring Regulations themselves (BS 7671) give little help. Suggestions of values for the allowances for diversity are given in Table 4.2. Distribution boards must not have diversity applied. They must be able to carry the total load connected to them.

It should be noted that Table 4.2 does not include suggestions for industrial situations. This is because there is such a wide variation in the arrangements and practices in such situations that it would be presumptive to assess diversity without an intimate knowledge of the situation. Note that no data are included for the domestic situation. This is because the Electricity at Work Regulations are not deemed to cover houses.

Perhaps the situation will be clearer with a worked example the calculations for which will be based on Table 4.2.

Example 4.1
A shop has the following single-phase loads, which are balanced as evenly as possible across the 415 V three-phase supply.

   3 x 6 kW and 7 x 3 kW thermostatically controlled water heaters
   2 x 6 kW instantaneous heaters
   1 x 6 kW and 2 x 4 kW cookers
   10 kW of discharge lighting (sum of tube ratings)
   10 x 30 A ring circuits feeding 13 A sockets.

Calculate the total demand of the system, assuming that diversity can be applied.

The single-phase voltage for a 415V three-phase system is $415/\sqrt{3} = 240$ V. All loads with the exception of the discharge lighting can be assumed to be at unity power factor, so current may be calculated from

$$I = \frac{P}{V}$$

Thus the current per kilowatt will be $\frac{1000}{240}$ A $= 4.17$ A

Water heaters (thermostatic)
No diversity is allowable, so the total load will be:
   $(3 \times 6) + (7 \times 3)$ kW $= 18 + 21$ kW $= 39$ kW
This gives a total single-phase current of I $= 39 \times 4.17 = 162.6$ A

Water heaters (instantaneous)
100% of largest plus 100% of next means that in effect there is no allowable diversity.
Single-phase current is thus $= 2 \times 6 \times 4.17 = 50.0\,A$

Cookers

100% of largest	=	$6 \times 4.17\,A$	=	25.0 A
80% of second	=	$\dfrac{80 \times 4 \times 4.17}{100}\,A$	=	13.3 A
60% of remainder	=	$\dfrac{60 \times 4 \times 4.17}{100}\,A$	=	10.0 A
Total for cookers	=	48.3 A		

Discharge lighting
90% of total which must be increased to allow for power factor and control gear losses.

Lighting current $= \dfrac{10 \times 4.17 \times 1.8 \times 90}{100}\,A = 67.6\,A$

Ring circuits

First circuit 100%, so current is			30 A
75% of remainder	= $\dfrac{9 \times 30 \times 75}{100}$	=	202.5 A
Total current demand for ring circuits		=	232.5 A
Total single phase current demand		=	561.0 A

If a perfect balance is assumed, three phase line current
$= \dfrac{561.0}{3}\,A = 187\,A$

Note on UK Voltage levels
Several years ago it was internationally agreed that voltage levels in the United Kingdom and the rest of Europe should be unified. The European standard voltage of 220 V (380 V for three-phase supplies) would be increased to 230 V (400 V three-phase) and the UK values should be reduced from 240 V (415 V)

to 230 V (400 V). Because the existing UK voltage levels were well within the allowable tolerances, the Supply Companies took the decision to maintain voltages unchanged. We thus have the somewhat ridiculous situation of having declared voltage levels of 230 V (400 V) when they are in fact 240 V (415 V).

It is very important that when calculating current levels, the **actual** voltages are used, as in the maximum demand calculation above. If the lower, nominal voltages are used, the resulting maximum demand values calculated would be lower than those that may actually occur. This could possibly result in specification of equipment which is unable to deal with the actual current flowing. Similar remarks apply to the calculation of currents for correct cable selection (4.4)

4.4   CORRECT CABLE SELECTION   (Regulation 5)

4.4.1   Introduction

It is a requirement of the Safety at Work Regulations 1989 that an electrical installation shall be so designed and installed that it will have a strength and capability to be safe in the use for which it is intended as well as being able safely to withstand fault conditions. It follows that the cables installed must be suitable for their intended purpose, so that they will not fail and cause danger to those in the work situation.

Increasingly, thermosetting insulation, consisting often of cross-linked polyethylene (XPLE), is being used for electrical installations. It may be safely used when the conductor temperature is up to 90°C. Cables usually fail as a result of becoming too hot, the weak point normally being the insulation. PVC is the most common insulation, and this material will soften with increasing temperature, allowing the cable cores to "migrate" through the material. Where a conductor presses against the PVC insulation, as it is likely to do at a cable bend, allowing the insulation to become too hot will eventually result in the conductor reaching its surface and making contact with the cable surroundings. If this is a metallic enclosure, such as steel trunking or conduit, a short circuit will result. For this reason, it is most important that normal grade PVC is not allowed to exceed its safe operating temperature of 70°C.

There are special types of PVC which may be used safely up to 85°C, and there are mineral insulated cables, which may reach a temperature of only 70°C when covered in PVC or in contact with combustible material, or may run at up to 105°C if bare, not likely to be touched and fixed to surfaces which cannot catch fire. The temperature reached by a cable in service depends on a number of factors which are considered in the following Sections.

4.4.2 Current carrying capacity

All cables have electrical resistance, so there must be an energy loss when they carry current, and this loss appears as heat. A cable of larger cross-sectional area will have smaller resistance, and will have a higher current rating. As heat is dissipated in the cable its temperature rises. As it does so, the heat it loses to its surroundings by conduction, convection and radiation also increases. The rate of heat loss is a function of the difference between the conductor temperature and that of the surroundings, so as the conductor temperature rises, so does the rate at which it loses heat.

A cable carrying a steady-state current, which produces a fixed heating effect, will get hotter until it reaches the balance temperature where heat input is equal to heat loss (*see* Fig. 4.1). The final temperature achieved by the cable will thus depend on the current carried, how easily heat is dissipated from the cable and the temperature of the cable surroundings. The safe limits for the current carrying capacity of various types of cable are given in the Tables of Appendix 4 of the IEE Wiring Regulations (BS 7671).

Since the cable temperature depends on the ability of the cable to shed heat it also depends on a number of other factors.

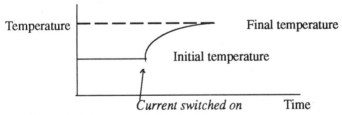

Figure 4.1 Heat balance curve for a cable

4.4.3 Ambient temperature

The transfer of heat, whether by conduction, convection or radiation, depends on temperature difference — heat flows from hot to cold at a rate which depends on the temperature difference between them. Thus, a cable installed near the roof of a boiler house where the surrounding (ambient) temperature is very high will not dissipate heat so readily as one clipped to the wall of a cold cellar.

To allow for this reduction in cooling in any situation where the ambient temperature exceeds 30°C, the cable must be derated. In practice this is done by multiplying the current carrying capacity by a factor which reduces as the ambient temperature increases, and which is found from Table 4C1 of the IEE Wiring Regulations (BS 7671). Lower correction factors, resulting in larger cables, apply where protection is by semi-enclosed (rewirable) fuses, and are shown in Table 4C2 of the IEE Wiring Regulations.

4.4.4 Thermal insulation

The use of thermal insulation in buildings, in the forms of cavity wall filling, roof space blanketing, and so on, is now a requirement of the Building Regulations. Since the purpose of such materials is to limit the transfer of heat, they will clearly affect the ability of a cable to dissipate the heat build up within it when in contact with them.

If a cable is in a wall cavity which is filled with thermal insulation, the correct current rating table from the IEE Regulations (Appendix 4) will make the necessary allowance by reducing the current carrying capacity. If the cable is in contact with insulation for more than 0.5 m of its length, where it is run in the insulation in a roof, for example, the current rating is halved by the application of a factor of 0.5. In some cases a cable is only surrounded by thermal insulation for a short length, such as where it passes through an insulated wall. In such a case the derating factor depends on the length enclosed in thermal insulation, and varies from 0.89 for 50 mm length to 0.55 for 400 mm (Table 52A of the IEE Wiring Regulations - BS 7671).

4.4.5 Grouping

If a number of cables is installed together and all are carrying current, they will all warm up. Those which are on the outside of the group will be able to transmit heat outwards, but will be restricted in losing heat inwards towards other warm cables. Cables 'buried' in others near the centre of the group may find it impossible to shed heat at all, and will rise further in temperature (Fig 4.2).

Because of this, cables installed in groups with others (for example, if enclosed in a conduit or trunking) are allowed to carry less current than similar cables clipped to, or lying on, a solid surface which can dissipate heat more easily. If surface mounted cables are touching, the reduction in the current rating is, as would be expected, greater than if they are separated.

A derating factor is applied to a group of cables, its value reducing as the number of cables in the group increases. The value ranges from 0.94 for two circuits where cables are spaced and clipped to a surface, to 0.38 for twenty bunched circuits. Exact data can be found from Table 4B1 of the IEE Wiring Regulations (BS 7671).

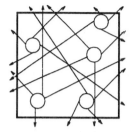 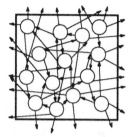

Figure 4.2 To illustrate the need for a derating factor for grouped cables

4.5 CORRECT SWITCH AND FUSE GEAR SELECTION (Regulation 5)

If cables are not to overheat under fault conditions, it follows that the protecting fuse or circuit breaker must cut off the current before the cable temperature becomes too high. This means correct selection of fuses and circuit breakers in relation to cable ratings, which have already been assessed as described in 4.4. Such selection requires the application of the time/current characteristics of fuses and circuit breakers. Characteristics for all standard protective devices are given in Appendix 3 of the IEE Wiring Regulations (BS 7671).

All fuses and circuit breakers should be capable of clearing the prospective short circuit current for the position at which they are installed. This is the current which would flow due to a short circuit fault between live conductors or from the phase to earth. Its value depends directly on the supply voltage, and varies inversely with the circuit impedance. Thus, the prospective short circuit current at the intake position of an installation close to a large supply substation may well be 25 kA (25,000 A), or it could be as low as 2 kA within a small installation remote from the supply substation.

The circuit protection (fuse or circuit breaker) and the cables protected must satisfy all the following conditions:

1.   the current rating of the protective device is not less than the circuit design current,

2.   the current rating of the protective device is not greater than that of the smallest cable protected, and

3.   the current to cause operation of the protective device is not more than 1.45 times the current carrying capacity of the smallest cable protected.

Rewirable fuses (strictly called semi-enclosed fuses) are still used to some extent in installations which are subject to the Electricity at Work Regulations. Such fuses are slower to clear faults and overloads, and the rating of such a fuse must not exceed 0.725 times the lowest current rating of any cable protected by them.

4.6 HAZARDOUS OR ADVERSE CONDITIONS (Regulation 6)

In some cases a work situation, and the electrical equipment installed in it, will be subject to adverse or hazardous conditions, requiring the designer of the electrical installation to choose special equipment which may have to be installed in a non-standard way. Examples are:

1.   installations and equipment for use out of doors, and thus subject to rain, snow, *etc*. The special precautions necessary for such an installation will also apply where it is possible that the building in which they are installed may not remain weatherproof,

2.   protection in the form of lightning conductors may be essential in some cases. Guidance will be found in BS 6651, Code of Practice for the protection of structures against lightning,

3.   cables in industrial situations which are run on the surface and which may need additional protection from risk of mechanical damage,

4.   changes in temperature may cause expansion and contraction to take

place, resulting in mechanical damage. An example is a very long straight run of conduit, which may buckle in hot weather or may pull apart at its joints in very low temperatures. The problem can be overcome by installing one or more changes in the direction of the run to form expansion loops,

5. very high humidity may require the installation of wiring systems and equipment which is non corrosive, for example by the use of galvanised steel. It is also important in these cases to avoid contact between dis-similar metals, such as steel and aluminium, which could otherwise lead to electrolytic corrosion,

6. dirty conditions may be a special hazard, in some instances dirt collecting within the enclosures to limit cooling, and in others providing a path for current conduction between live parts. Regular cleaning becomes a necessity in these situations,

7. in some cases a corrosive atmosphere may cause damage to structural metalwork of equipments, to conducting systems within them, or to insulators. Again, regular cleaning is required, although in severe cases the cubicles protecting electrical equipment may need to be pressurised to prevent the entry of the corrosive atmosphere,

8. layers of combustible dust on electrical equipment may cause a fire hazard, or the presence of clouds of dust may give rise to the possibility of explosion. Regular cleaning, or prevention of entry of dust will usually solve the problem,

9. in the event of a fault it is not unusual for electrical equipment to become hot or even to emit sparks. Thus it is essential to ensure that flammable materials are not kept close to such equipment,

10. agricultural and horticultural situations, where electrical installations and equipment may need protection from water sprays or jets, high humidity, animals, and so on,

11. construction sites, where the temporary nature of the installation as well as adverse conditions of water, mud and so on create special hazards. The distribution of electricity in such situations is the subject of BS CP

1017 and Health and Safety Executive publication GS 24, and

12.   situations such as mines, oil refineries, gas terminals and the like, where there may be a potentially explosive atmosphere. Electrical equipment for use in such situations is covered by HS(G) 22 and BS 5345.

Electric shock is always worse where the voltage level is higher, so it follows that its effects can be less severe if a lower voltage is used. The IEE Wiring Regulations (BS 7671) refer to such a voltage as "extra-low", and whilst its use will often prevent dangerous electric shock, it will lead to the need for larger conductors to carry the higher currents required to provide a given power.

Equipment for use in conditions where it may be subjected to moisture or to dust and other solid particles must be suitably protected. A method of indicating the degree of protection from water or mechanical objects is the index of protection (IP) indicated in BS 5490. A piece of equipment which has protection is given an IP rating which consists of two numbers. The first shows the protection afforded from mechanical objects, and the second from water. Thus, an enclosure to IP43 is protected from solid objects of up to 1 mm in diameter and from spraying water.

If one of the two forms of protection is not provided the number concerned is replaced with X. A very common classification for electrical equipment is IP2X, mechanical protection against a solid object of diameter less than 12 mm (for instance, a human finger) but with no water protection. Table 4.3 shows details of the IP system.

4.7   JOINTS AND CONNECTIONS   (Regulation 10)

All joints and connections in an electrical system, whether temporary or permanent, are required to be mechanically and electrically suitable for the use for which they are intended. IEE Wiring Regulation 13-6 is very similar to Regulation 10 of the Electricity at Work Regulations. The Regulation applies to circuit and to protective conductors under both normal and fault conditions, whether that fault occurs in the joint or connection itself or elsewhere in the system. For example, a cable connector may be quite satisfac-

tory when carrying no more than its rated current of 16 A, but could it fail
if subjected to overload current of 30 A.

Table 4.3 Numbers in the I P system

First number	Mechanical protection against	Second number	Water protection against
0	Not protected	0	Not protected
1	Solid objects exceeding 50 mm	1	Dripping water
2	Solid objects exceeding 12 mm	2	Dripping water when tilted up to 15°
3	Solid objects exceeding 2.5 mm	3	Spraying water
4	Solid objects exceeding 1.0 mm	4	Splashing water
5	Dust protected	5	Water jets
6	Dust tight	6	Heavy seas
		7	Effects of immersion
		8	Submersion

Plugs and sockets must be so arranged that it is impossible for a person using them to come into contact with live connections. Examples are the insulated sleeves applied to the base of 13 A plug pins to prevent contact with live pins during insertion or removal, and the need for a male and female connector to have the female side connected to the supply so that the exposed pins of the male side are never live (*see* Fig 6.10). If a protective (earthing) connection is included in a plug and socket system, it should be arranged so that the protective system is closed before the live conductors when making, and opened after the live conductors when breaking.

Particular care is needed when dealing with connections for portable equipment, because such plugs and sockets are likely to be used frequently, often by unskilled people who will not appreciate the dangers present. Health and Safety publications dealing with the safety of portable appliances are PM 32, PM 38, GS 23 and GS 37.

4.8   PROTECTION AGAINST EXCESS CURRENT (Regulation 11)

4.8.1   Impossibility of preventing excess current

It must be made clear that it is almost impossible totally to prevent excess current from flowing. It takes time for a protective device to operate — for example, an 80 A cartridge fuse to BS 1361 will take more than 300 s (5 minutes) to open when carrying a current of 200 A — and during this time the excess current will flow without hindrance from the protection system. Neither is it possible to prevent electric shock entirely in the event of a fault. For example, the IEE Wiring Regulations (BS 7671) require that in the event of an earth fault on a piece of portable equipment the supply should be disconnected by the protection system in less than 0.4 s. However, during this time it is not impossible for the user of the faulty equipment to be subjected to the full supply voltage. As we shall indicate in Chapter 6, although the victim will receive a shock in this case, it is very unlikely to be fatal.

There may also be instances where cutting off the fault current could result in greater danger than if it were allowed to continue for a short while. For example, a lifting electromagnet in a scrap yard could drop its load onto people below in the event of a fuse blowing due to overload. An overload alarm would allow time for the load to be lowered or moved to a safe position before switching the circuit off.

It is necessary to anticipate the abnormal conditions which could result in excess current. For example, precautions may need to be taken to prevent the mechanical overloading of an electric motor which would result in an excessive overload current.

4.8.2 Faults requiring protection

There is a number of types of fault from which protection is required, including:

1.   overload currents, caused in practice by a load being applied which is greater than the design value for the circuit concerned. This could be due to a failure in the assessment of diversity, too many appliances being plugged in to a ring circuit, an electric motor being required to provide an output larger than expected, and so on

2.   short circuit currents which will occur when a short circuit or very low impedance appears between conductors with different voltage levels. The fault may be from phase to phase of a three-phase system (note that the term "phase" has now replaced "live" as far as the IEE Wiring Regulations   (BS 7671) are concerned), or from phase to neutral. The reason for the short circuit may be a cable fault, external damage to the wiring system, and so on

3.   earth faults, due to a short circuit or a low impedance between phase and the protective or earth system. If a residual current device (RCD) is fitted, this will remove the supply quickly when the fault occurs. RCDs are considered in greater detail in Section 6.7.8.

4.8.3 Selection of protection

A number of factors need to be considered when chosing a protective device, which will include:

1.   the type of equipment fed by the circuit,

2.   the kind of circuit concerned, for example, if a ring circuit,

3.   the earthing arrangement of the system, and

4.   the environment in which the protective device and the circuit are situated. For example, different solutions may be necessary for circuits with similar current requirements, one situated in an office and another in a steel-works.

4.9 SWITCHING OFF AND ISOLATION   (Regulation 12)

A basic requirement for the safety of any electrical system is that it should be possible to switch it off and to isolate it from its source of supply. As far as these Regulations are concerned, we only deal with switching off and isolating to prevent danger, although there may well be operational reasons additional to those of safety, such as the control of a motor or the operation of a lighting system. It must also be appreciated that the action of switching off can itself create danger in the form of arcing at the breaking contacts if an overload or fault is present.

We must first appreciate the basic difference between switching off and isolating. Switching off may well involve the breaking of normal load current (or even the higher current due to overload or short circuit) whereas isolation is concerned with cutting the already dead circuit so that reclosing the switch will not make it live again. Whilst a switch must be able to break currents, an isolator need not be designed to do so because it should only be operated after the current has been broken.

From a safety point of view, the isolator is just as important as the switch, because any person working on an isolated circuit or piece of equipment must be certain that it will not unexpectedly become live. To this end, an isolator must:

1.   be positioned so that it is always accessible to those who need to use it,

2.   be clearly marked to indicate the circuits and systems that will be isolated by its operation,

3.   be arranged so that unauthorised or unexpected reclosing is not possible. This means that the isolator must be provided with a means of locking in the "off" position, with a key which can be retained by the person at work

on the circuit or the equipment. Padlocks may be used but may sometimes not be secure because of interference; there has been a case of an accident which happened because a worker hacksawed a padlock to enable him to restore the supply to his machine! Sometimes an isolator has a handle which can be removed only in the "off" position and retained by the worker,

4.   be capable of completely separating the system or the circuit concerned from the source of electrical power. This means that the clearance between contacts should be at least that required by the appropriate British Standard and have adequate creepage and clearance distances which will ensure that the isolation gap cannot fail electrically, and

5.   be able to isolate more than one system or piece of equipment where it is appropriate for the group of systems and/or equipments to be isolated simultaneously.

5
Access and Lighting

5.1 INTRODUCTION (Regulation 15)

When choosing the position of electrical equipment, safety is improved if adequate working space is provided. It must also be possible to gain access to the equipment without endangering the worker concerned, and there must be enough light to enable the required work to be carried out. There is an absolute duty on the employer to ensure that these three requirements are met.

5.2 ACCESS AND WORKING SPACE (Regulation 15)

All electrical equipment must be easily reached by those who need to work on it. Not only does this mean that switch and fusegear which is available from floor level must remain unimpeded with rubbish, stored equipment, etc, but special means may be necessary to ensure safe access to equipment installed in difficult positions. Thus the lighting equipment of an aircraft hanger, which will be at high level and remote from walls which could safely be used to support ladders, may need to be provided with lowering gear so that it can be repaired or serviced at ground level. Alternatively, an adequate platform may be provided to allow safe and secure access to the lighting in its operating position. If the latter method is used, it may also be necessary to institute working procedures which prevent the possibility of collision between the access platform and vehicles, such as aircraft.

The provision of the spaces specified in Table 5.1 must not be assumed to allow live working, which must always be avoided unless absolutely necessary.

Special attention must be given to switchgear and other equipment where live working may be necessary. The Regulation specifies adequate access without giving the required spacing. However, the Memorandum of Guidance refers to Regulation 17 of the Electricity (Factories Act) Special Regulations, 1908 and 1944. Although produced many years ago, these requirements could still be used in a legal action against those thought to be flouting the current Regulation 15. The height and width of access in front of a switchboard are related to the highest operating voltage concerned, and are given in Table 5.1. It will be appreciated that when the Regulation was framed, Great Britain used only Imperial measurements, which have been shown in the Table as well as their metric counterparts.

Table 5.1 Minimum spaces in front of switchboards
(Taken from Regulation 17 of the Electricity (Factories Act) Special Regulations 1908 and 1944)

Voltage level of switchboard	Minimum height	Minimum width
Up to 650 V	7 ft (2.1 m)	3 ft (0.91 m)
Above 650 V	8 ft (2.4 m)	3 ft 6 in (1.07 m)

Where exposed conductors are present on both sides of the passageway, minimum width requirements must be increased.

The spaces specified are where there could be exposed live conductors, and are intended to provide enough space to enable those working:

1. to pull back away from the live conductors without hindrance, and

2. to pass each other with ease and without pushing the person working on the live system.

Switchgear should be housed in special switchrooms or cupboards which are large enough to allow walk-in access, so as to give proper working space, and to enable the space to be locked to prevent unauthorised entry. Where there is a possibility of switchgear being subject to live working, the clearances specified in Table 5.1 will apply. It is important that where switch and fusegear are installed in a cupboard, working space is maintained around them. Switchrooms should not be used for storage or as workshops. It is important that a proper system of maintenance of the space around switchboards should be effected to ensure that the area remains clear and uncluttered. Defining areas with painted floors may help in this respect.

In some cases, access will be needed to current transformers, cable boxes, and so on, which are situated at the back of a switchboard. In such a case, the clearances stated in Table 5.1 must be provided both in front of and behind the switchboard.

The Regulations themselves do not specifically require space to allow speedy and safe evacuation from an area in the event of a fault, a fire, or other difficulty. However the need for such space is specified in the Health and Safety at Work Act (Section 2(2)(d)).

5.3 LIGHTING (Regulation 15)

It will be obvious that safety will be improved if people can see clearly. In order to do this there must be sufficient illumination. Ideally a good level of natural light will be best, but artificial lighting will become necessary at times. It will be appreciated that an artificial lighting level which is adequate for the general workplace may be insufficient for work on electrical apparatus.

Since the artificial lighting itself is almost certain to be electrical, it may be lost in the event of an electrical fault which will necessitate attention to the electrical system. It follows that emergency lighting will be needed in this case. The Regulations do not say that a full emergency lighting system is necessary, so uninterrupible power supplies (UPS), emergency handlamps or torches will be acceptable, provided that they give sufficient illumination to prevent danger.

Lighting levels are stated in HS(G) 38 "Lighting at work". A level of 100 lux (100 lumens per square metre) should be sufficient for most maintenance and repair work, with a minimum of 50 lux. It is important to appreciate that these lighting levels must apply on the plane of the work. For example, an overhead light may well provide sufficient illumination of the floor in front of a switchboard, but the lighting level on the equipment itself may be insufficient due to the oblique angle at which the light reaches it. It is also important to take account of shadows when designing a lighting system. For example, a vertical switchboard may be well lit by a light in front of it. However, the worker will also have to be in front of the board, and his shadow may prevent good lighting of the task.

6
Electric Shock Protection

6.1 THE SHOCK DANGER (Regulation 2)

Burns are a constant hazard for those working on, or with, electrical equipment, but the biggest danger of all is electric shock. Before considering the methods for reducing the danger of shock, it will be useful to consider the nature of shock.

The nervous system of the human body controls all its movements, both conscious and unconscious. The system carries electrical signals between the brain and the muscles, which are thus stimulated into action. The signals are electro-chemical in nature, with levels of a few millivolts, so when the human body becomes part of a much more powerful external circuit, its normal operations are swamped by the outside signals. The current forced through the nervous system of the body by external voltage is electric shock.

All the muscles affected receive much stronger signals than those they normally get and operate very much more violently as a result. This causes uncontrolled movements and pain. Even a shock victim who is still conscious is usually quite unable to counter the effects of the shock, because the signals from his brain, which try to offset the effects of the shock currents, are lost in the strength of the imposed signals.

A good example is the 'no-let-go' effect. Here, a person touches a conductor which sends shock currents through his hand. The muscles respond by closing the fingers on the conductor, so it is tightly grasped. The person wants to release the conductor, which is causing pain, but the electrical signals from his brain are swamped by the shock current, and he is unable to let go of the offending conductor.

The effects of an electric shock vary considerably depending on the current imposed on the nervous system, and the path taken through the body. This subject is very complex but it has become clear that the damage done to the human body depends on four factors:

1. the value of shock current flowing, and

2. the time for which it flows, and

3. the path through the body which the current takes, and

4. the supply frequency, if it is alternating.

These four factors have governed the international movement towards making electrical installations safer.

6.2 WHEN IS ELECTRIC SHOCK DANGEROUS?

In simple terms the human body can be considered as a circuit through which an applied potential difference will drive a current. The current flowing will depend on the voltage applied and the resistance of the current path. Of course, we should try to prevent or to limit shock by aiming to stop a dangerous potential difference from being applied across the body. However, we have to accept that there are times when this is impossible, so the important factor becomes the resistance of the current path.

The human body is composed largely of water, and has very low resistance. The skin, however, has very high resistance, the value depending on its nature, on the possible presence of water, and on whether it has become burned. Thus, most of the resistance to the passage of current through the human body is at the points of entry and exit through the skin. A person with naturally hard and dry skin will offer much higher resistance to shock current than one with soft and moist skin; the skin resistance becomes very low if it has been burned, because of the presence of conducting particles of carbon.

Figure 6.1 is a simplified representation of the shock path through the body, with an equivalent circuit which indicates the components of the resistance concerned. It must be appreciated that the diagram is very approximate; the flow of current through the body will, for example, cause the victim to sweat, reducing the resistance of the skin very quickly after the shock commences. The opposition to the flow of current is also affected by other factors, such as the applied voltage, the state of health of the victim, and so on. Fortunately, it is not often that people at work who are using electrical installations have bare feet, and the resistance of the footwear, as well as of the floor coverings, will often increase overall shock path resistance and may reduce shock current.

Full details of the latest knowledge concerning electric shock and its effects will be found in BS PD 6519.

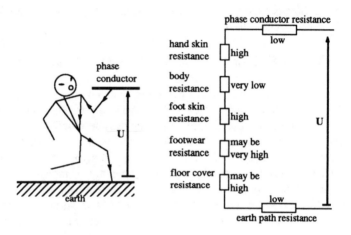

Fig 6.1   Path of electric shock current

6.3   SEVERITY OF AN ELECTRIC SHOCK

There are few reliable figures for shock current effects, because they differ from person to person, and for a particular person, with time and with the environment. However, we know that something over one milliampere of current in the body produces the sensation of shock, and that one hundred milliamperes is likely quickly to prove fatal, particularly if it passes through the heart.

If a shock persists, its effects are likely to prove to be more dangerous. For example, a shock current of 500 mA may have no lasting ill effects if its duration is less than 20 ms, but 50 mA for 10 s could well prove to be fatal. A properly designed and installed electrical installation will contain protective devices (circuit breakers and fuses) which will cut off the supply quickly in the event of a fault which could cause shock. For circuits feeding sockets, where the contact between the shock victim and the apparatus is likely to be good, this will be within 0.4 s. For fixed equipment, which will probably not be grasped tightly, it is within 5 s.

The effects of the shock will vary, but the most dangerous results are ventricular fibrillation (where the heart beat sequence is disrupted) and compression of the chest, resulting in a failure to breathe. Ventricular fibrillation is most likely when the supply is alternating at a frequency of 50 Hz. It is important to remove the effect causing the shock from the victim as soon as possible. This is best done by switching off the circuit concerned quickly, or by dragging the victim away from contact. This must be done using something which is non-conductive, such as dry clothing, or there is a danger that the rescuer will become another victim! If the patient is not breathing, artificial respiration should be started at once, and continued until qualified help arrives.

6.4   DIRECT AND INDIRECT CONTACT

As far as the IEE Wiring Regulations are concerned there are two ways in which a person can make contact with a live system and so get a shock.

1   Direct contact
An electric shock results from contact with a conductor which forms part of a circuit and would be expected to be live. A typical example would be if someone removed the plate from a switch and touched the live conductors inside (*see* Fig 6.2).

2   Indirect contact
An electric shock is received from contact with a part of the electrical installation which would not normally be expected to be live, but has become

so as the result of a fault. This would be termed an exposed conductive part. Alternatively, a shock may be received from a conducting part which is totally unconnected with the electrical installation, but which has become live as the result of a fault. Such a part would be called an extraneous conductive part.

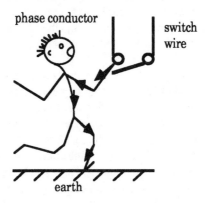

phase conductor

switch
wire

earth

Fig 6.2 Direct contact

An example illustrating both types of indirect contact is shown in Fig 6.3. Danger in this situation results from the presence of a phase to earth fault on the kettle. This makes the kettle case live, so that contact with it, and with a good earth (in this case the tap) makes the human body part of the shock circuit if the kettle protective (earthing) system were ineffective.

6.5 SYSTEM CONSTRUCTION AND MAINTENANCE (Regulation 4)
6.5.1 Construction (Regulation 4)
The term "construction" in this Regulation must be taken to mean the design of the electrical system, the manner of its installation and the component parts which together make up the complete installation. In designing the system, regard must be paid to all likely, or reasonably foreseeable, conditions applying to its use which could affect the safety of those using it. In particular, the design should take account of:

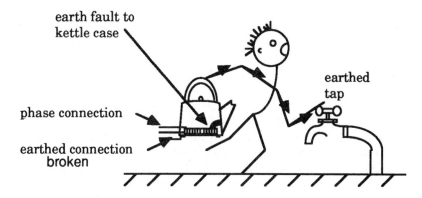

Fig 6.3   Indirect contact

1.   the load and the probable fault conditions,
2.   the rating of the equipment used,
3.   the need for suitable fuses and/or circuit breakers,
4.   the environmental conditions applying, such as the presence of water, dust, etc. which will affect the type of protection needed,
5.   the fault level at the supply position and the ability of the protective system to cope with such faults,
6.   the special needs of the users of the installation, and
7.   the way in which testing, commissioning and maintenance are likely to be carried out.

It should be borne in mind that the safety of the complete system is dependent on the correct operation of each of the separate parts. For example, where step-up transformers are used, special care will be necessary to prevent the higher secondary voltage from appearing on the lower voltage primary circuits.

6.5.2 Maintenance (Regulation 4)
Proper and effective maintenance must be carried out regularly to ensure that the initial safety level of a system is maintained, and it is also important to ensure that the maintenance itself is carried out safely. The frequency of the maintenance, and its quality, must be chosen to ensure that the system is

always safe so far as is reasonably practicable.

Preventive maintenance will require the keeping of proper test records which include test results and dates, from which an impending failure may be forecast. Such records will also be useful if it becomes necessary to demonstrate that a proper schedule of maintenance has been followed. Details of Health and Safety Executive suggestions for testing and test equipment will be found in their publications HS(G) 13 and GS 38.

It is vitally important that maintenance should be carried out wherever possible on an electrical system which has been made dead. Having switched off a system, it must be tested to ensure that it is really dead using an instrument which has had its operation proved immediately before use.

There will be cases where it is impossible to make an electrical system dead before working on it. Examples include earth fault loop impedance measurement, fault finding, some types of testing and live jointing in supply systems. In such cases it is very important indeed that the work is only carried out by people who have been fully trained and are experienced so that they appreciate the dangers concerned and the procedures to be followed to avoid danger.

In some cases, non-electrical workers may be in danger from electrical systems. For example, there may be considerable risk of danger for those carrying out excavations near buried cables, or operating mobile cranes close to overhead lines. In fact, half the fatalities due to electric shock are usually as a result of contact with overhead lines. Problems such as these can often be reduced by good working practices, such as a careful search of plans showing the routes of buried cables before excavation commences, or erecting "goal posts" limiting access for high vehicles close to overhead lines.

6.5.3 Periodic inspection and testing (Regulation 4)
An electrical installation must be properly tested and certified safe after its initial construction, as required by the IEE Wiring Regulations (BS 7671). In most cases the initial installation contract will specify that the installer is responsible for faults occurring during the first six or twelve months of its life, but all too often there is no system which ensures that the installation is subsequently inspected and tested. The IEE Wiring Regulations do require the installer to tell his customer when another inspection and test is due, and also insist that he posts a durable notice at the mains position giving the same information.

Table 6.1 Suggested intervals between periodic tests and inspections

Type of installation	Maximum period between inspections
Agricultural and horticultural	3 years
Caravans	3 years
Caravan sites	1 year* or 3 years* if the supply system is underground
Churches	5 years
Cinemas	1 year*
Commercial premises	5 years
Construction sites	3 years
Domestic premises	10 years
Educational establishments	5 years
Emergency lighting	3 years
Fire alarm systems	1 year
Highway power supplies	6 years
Hospitals	5 years
Industrial premises	3 years
Launderettes	1 year*
Leisure complexes, etc.	1 year
Marinas	1 year
Petrol filling stations	1 year*
Public houses	5 years
Restaurants and hotels	1 year
Temporary installations	3 months
Theatres, etc	1 year*

Where maximum periods are marked * there is a legal requirement for retests at these intervals

All too often the good intentions of those responsible will be forgotten in the years that follow, so that it is not unusual for the electrical installation to remain untested for many years, unless, of course, a fault or an accident calls belated attention to the need to test. During its life, an electrical installation may deteriorate due to normal ageing, may have substandard additions installed, or may be damaged. Any of these problems would come to light in a periodic inspection and test, which is therefore essential.

How often is this inspecting and testing process necessary? The Electricity at Work Regulations 1989 are not forthcoming with this information, simply referring to other publications which often do not lay down the intervals required. Sensible time intervals between inspection and testing of electrical installations are suggested in Table 6.1. In a few cases, which are clearly marked, this testing is compulsory, so it must be carried out.

6.6   PREVENTING DIRECT CONTACT (Regulation 7)

6.6.1 Introduction

A major method of avoiding electric shock is to make sure that people will not come into contact with live conductors (direct contact). This can be done in a number of ways, including:

1.   providing the conductors with effective insulation,

2.   placing the conductors so that they are out of reach of people,

3.   protecting the conductors with barriers or enclosures, and

4.   erecting obstacles which prevent people from getting close to conductors.

6.6.2 Provision of insulation (Regulation 7)

The use of insulated conductors is, perhaps, the most obvious method of preventing contact with live conductors. Not only will such insulation be capable of preventing electric shock, but will also prevent contact between conductors at different potentials (phase to phase, phase to neutral, or phase to earth) which could result in arcing, fire or explosion.

It follows that the type and grade of insulation used must be suitable for the situation and for the voltage concerned. To ensure that the insulation is not damaged in normal service, it often requires protection using conduit, trunking or steel armouring. Further detail on this subject will be found in the IEE Wiring Regulations (BS 7671) and in the various British Standards for different types of cables.

6.6.3 Placing conductors out of reach (Regulation 7)

For overhead lines, the Electricity Supply Regulations 1988 require that for voltages up to and including 33 kV the clearance should be 5.2 m, increased to 5.8 m where there is access for vehicles.

Other live conductors should be at least "beyond arm's reach". Figure 6.4 (based on the IEE Wiring Regulations (BS 7671)) gives a plan and an elevation to specify the limit of arm's reach for systems up to 1000 V.

The outer lines on the diagrams indicate the limit of reach assumed possible for a person using the space shown. Great care must be taken by the designer and the installer if placing out of reach is to be used to allow the application of uninsulated conductors. Although not normally reached by a person, the use in some circumstances of long conducting devices, such as metal tubes, ladders, or access towers (possibly during maintenance or decorating operations) may give rise to danger.

6.6.4 Providing barriers or enclosures (Regulation 7)

The use of enclosures is the standard method for protection. For example, a circuit breaker board will be provided with an enclosing box which not only keeps the interior free from dust but also prevents people from making contact with live connections. Where the voltage concerned is no greater than 1000 V, the top surface of the enclosure must be protected to IP4X (impossible to push in a tool or wire more than 1 mm thick) and the rest of the enclosure to IP2X (protection against contact by a standard finger).

6.6.5 Protection by provision of obstacles (Regulation 7)

This method is used to prevent people from unintentionally being close enough to live parts to make contact with them. For example, an exterior substation may be provided with a high fence to prevent people straying into a dangerous area. When work is being done within a normally available space, or where testing of an electrical installation is being carried out, movable fences or partitions may be used to alert people to the danger of entering an area. Such obstacles should usually be provided with notices to draw attention to the danger of entering a dangerous area. Consideration should be given to the use of pictorial warnings or of more secure barriers where it is possible that those who use the area may be unable to read the notices.

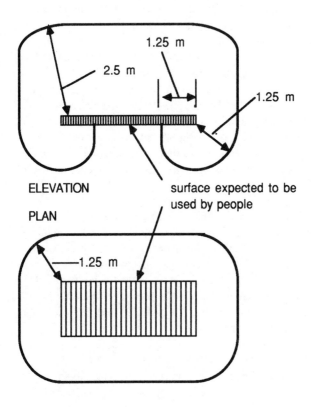

ELEVATION

PLAN

surface expected to be
used by people

Figure 6.4 Arm's reach for systems of up to 1000 V

6.7 EARTHING   (Regulation 8)
6.7.1 Introduction
Regulation 8 refers to the danger arising from a conductor, which would not
normally be live, in the event of it becoming so. Conductors which are normally live are those which are expected to carry current, so we are looking

here at conductors which are normally current-free. Such conductors could include the protective (earthing) system, any other metalwork, such as structural steelwork, ducting, water and central heating pipework and radiators, the metallic bodies of electric motors, all metalwork of machines like lathes, guillotines, shapers, *etc.* and so on. They may also be in the forms of gas, liquid or plasma.

The protective measures which can be taken include:

1. earthing and equipotential bonding,
2. isolated or separated systems,
3. earth free non-conducting locations,
4. the limitation of current and hence of energy,
5. connection to a common voltage reference point,
6. use of reduced voltage systems,
7. use of residual current devices (RCDs), and
8. use of double insulation.

6.7.2 Earthing and equipotential bonding (Regulation 8)

This is the most common method of protection, and involves connecting together all non-current carrying metalwork to form a zone within which it is not possible for exposed metalwork to be at different voltage levels which could cause a shock. This creates what is called an earthed equipotential zone, within which there is no danger because in the event of a fault the protective system cuts off the supply within a safe time as far as electric shock is concerned.

To create such a zone, it is necessary to connect (bond) together:

1. exposed conductive parts. These are metal parts of an electrical installation, such as conduits, switchgear casings, and so on, which are not normally live but which may become so under fault conditions, and

2. extraneous conductive parts. This term refers to all the conducting systems or parts which may introduce an electrical potential, usually earth potential, although they are not a part of the electrical system. Included would be structural steelwork, metal pipes and radiators of a heating system, pipework for hot and cold water supplies, and so on.

The object is to connect all parts together. If connected together with a conductor of sufficiently large cross-section, it is impossible for a high voltage difference to occur between them, thus providing safety. The cross-sectional areas of the bonding conductors must be sufficient to prevent a high volt drop across the conductor when it carries the expected current in the event of a fault. A larger cross-sectional area conductor will have lower resistance and hence a lower voltage drop when carrying a given amount of current. It is important that the requirements of the IEE Wiring Regulations (BS 7671) are fully implemented in this respect.

6.7.3 Isolated or separated systems (Regulation 8)

The object here is to create a zone within which there is no earthed metalwork which could form part of a shock circuit. Such a requirement is difficult to achieve, and even more difficult to maintain. The installation of new circuits, of water systems, or of any other metalwork can easily defeat the system. Thus, it is best applied very sparingly, the most usual application being in test houses or repair shops for electronic equipments, such as television receivers, which must be powered during fault tracing.
Precautions to be taken will include:

1.   all supplies should be taken through a double-wound isolating transformer,
2.   the resistance of all insulating floors and walls to earth should be greater than 50 kΩ (50,000 Ω),
3.   the supply voltage should be less than 500 V,
4.   extraneous conductive parts, such as building reinforcing metalwork, should be avoided as they could also provide an earth path,
5.   mains supplies which are not isolated must not be brought into the area. Thus, an appliance must not be used in the isolated area if fed from a socket situated outside it, and
6.   warning notices must be posted at every access to the area to draw attention to the dangers of providing connections to earth or of "im porting" unisolated electrical supplies.

A possible problem here is that a fault may remove the isolation of the system by connecting it to earth. If this happens, the safety of the isolated system is lost, probably without those using the area being aware of it, so that a second fault could have very dangerous consequences. The extra precautions which may be necessary to prevent this danger could include :

1. bonding all metal-work which can be touched,
2. the installation of an earth-fault detection system, which gives warn ing of the occurrence of the first fault,
3. using an insulation monitor to warn of any insulation failure, and
4. using an earth-free non-conducting environment.

Analysis of the isolated or separated system leads inevitably to the conclusion that its advantages are doubtful except in very specialised areas, such as those used for research, test houses and so on.

6.7.4 Earth-free non-conducting locations (Regulation 8)

In the case of indirect contact, the return path through earth forms an essential part of the electric shock circuit. If we remove the earth altogether, there can be no shocks due to indirect contact.

This may mean the total absence of metalwork or of other conducting materials, or will mean that all such materials must be bonded securely together and isolated from earth. It is easier to construct such an area of entirely insulating materials, when it will become a non-conducting location. Like the isolated system, this very specialised type of electrical installation is usually limited to test and research areas.

6.7.5 Current and energy limitation (Regulation 8)

In the event of electric shock, the amount of damage to the human nervous system depends on the external electrical energy dissipated in it. Energy depends, in this case, on the square of the current and the time for which it flows, thus, if the current is very small, or if it is allowed to flow for only a very short time, there can be no danger. It must be stressed that whilst there is no physical shock danger, sudden reactions on receiving the shock could lead to other types of danger. For example, a person on a ladder who receives such a shock may lose balance and fall. Thus there is no "safe" value of shock current, because even a very small value can cause an accident. Serious danger from the shock itself is unlikely to result, however, with a shock current of less than 5 mA (five thousandths of an ampere).

All electricians will be familiar, for example, with the battery-operated insulation resistance tester (often called a "Megger"). This device produces a high voltage for testing, but a shock from such a source, although painful, will not be lethal. This is because the instrument has high internal impedance, so that as soon as significant current starts to flow the internal volt drop reduces the shock voltage, and because the battery contains too little energy to provide a dangerously high current.

6.7.6   Connection to a common reference point (Regulation 8)

If there is always a common reference point for voltage, the value of which can be easily measured then its potential for causing danger is known. In the UK it is standard practice to earth the star point of the final distribution transformer so that the neutral of all supplies will be at, or nearly at, earth potential. In a supply fed from a protective multiple earth (PME) supply system, the neutral is also connected to earth at multiple points along the supply network.

Safety thus depends on always being sure that earth and the neutral of the supply are at the same potential, so that the voltage of other systems may be measured with reference to the earth and neutral. Any difference in potential between earth and neutral will never be more than a few volts, which cannot cause shock danger. Compare this situation with that in a normal office situation where a high potential arises following the build up of static charge on a person due to friction between his feet and a carpet of man-made material. When the charged person touches a metal filing cabinet, the static energy will be discharged, causing a shock, and often a spark. In this case there is no common voltage reference point.

6.7.7   Reduced voltage system (Regulation 8)

The severity of electric shock depends on the current flowing in the victim, which, in turn, depends on the voltage driving it. It follows that if the voltage is reduced, so too will be the shock danger. The use of reduced voltages is particularly effective where portable appliances are in use in wet or otherwise highly-conductive situations, such as on construction sites and in large pipes or boilers.

Whilst it is untrue to say that 50 V to earth is always a safe voltage, its use will significantly reduce danger. A standard method for feeding portable appliances on construction sites is through a double-wound step-down transformer with an output voltage of 110 V which has its secondary winding centre tap earthed. In this way, 110 V will be available to the appliance, but contact with either phase conductor can never result in a shock of more than 55 V to earth, as shown in Figure 6.5.

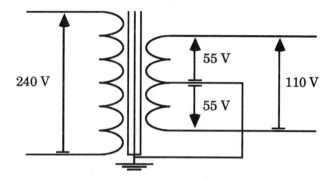

Figure 6.5   Transformer for safety supply to a portable appliance

It will be appreciated that the lower the voltage, the less the shock risk. We might be forgiven, therefore, for thinking that, for example, all supplies should be at 6 V. However, we must appreciate that to provide a given power, any reduction in voltage requires an increase in current. Use of 6 V, instead of 240 V, supplies, would mean that all our current levels would be increased forty times! This would require very large conductors to carry the heavy current, which would be totally uneconomic, and even then it is unlikely that conductors could be large enough to prevent a high conductor volt drop which would reduce the appliance voltage to the point where operation was inefficient.

Reduced voltage systems are in common use where danger would otherwise be present. Such supplies are almost always from the supply system using a step-down transformer, which may feed a fixed installation of non-standard sockets, or may be portable and intended to feed only one appliance.

6.7.8   Residual current devices (Regulation 8)
The RCD is a circuit breaker which continuously compares the current in

the phase with that in the neutral. The difference between the two (the residual current) will be flowing to earth, because it has left the supply through the phase and has not returned in the neutral *(see* Figure 6.6). There will always be some residual current in the insulation resistance and capacitance to earth, but in a healthy circuit such current will be low, seldom exceeding 2 mA.

The purpose of the residual current device is to monitor the residual current and to switch off the circuit quickly if it rises to a preset level. The arrangement of an RCD is shown in simplified form in Figure 6.7. The main contacts are closed against the pressure of a spring, which provides the energy to open them when the device trips. Phase and neutral currents pass through identical coils wound in opposing directions on a magnetic circuit, so that each coil will provide equal but opposing numbers of ampere turns when there is no residual current. The opposing ampere turns will cancel, and no magnetic flux will be set up in the magnetic circuit.

Residual earth current passes to the circuit through the phase coil but returns through the earth path, thus avoiding the neutral coil, which will therefore carry less current. This means that phase ampere turns exceed neutral ampere turns and an alternating magnetic flux results in the core. This flux links with the search coil, which is also wound on the magnetic circuit, inducing an e.m.f. in it. The value of this e.m.f. depends on the residual current, so it will drive a current to the tripping system which depends on the difference between phase and neutral currents. When the amount of residual current, and hence of tripping current, reaches a predetermined level, the circuit breaker trips, opening the main contacts and interrupting the circuit.

For circuit breakers operating at low residual current values, an amplifier may be used in the trip circuit. Since the sum of the currents in the phases and neutral of a three-phase supply with no earth current is always zero, the system can be used just as effectively with three-phase supplies. In high current circuits, it is more usual for the phase and neutral conductors to simply pass through the magnetic core instead of through coils wound on it

Operation depends on a mechanical system, which could possibly become stiff when old or dirty. Thus, regular testing is needed, and the RCD is provided with a test button which provides the rated level of residual current to ensure that the circuit breaker will operate. All RCDs are required to display a notice which draws attention to the need for frequent testing which can be carried out by the user, who presses a test button, usually marked T.

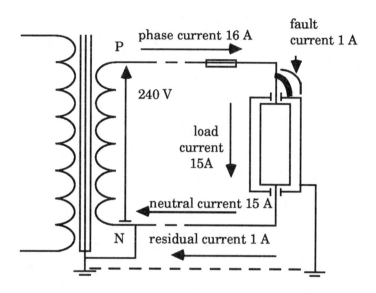

Fig 6.6 The meaning of the term residual current

The RCD can have a wide variety of operating currents. Usually these vary from 1 mA to 500 mA, the latter type being used for protection against fire rather than against shock. Since a shock current of 1 mA is safe, why not protect all our installations with 1 mA rated RCDs and thus prevent death from shock altogether? The answer is that the normal leakage to earth from an installation, due to current flow through the insulation and through earth capacitances, is usually higher than this figure, so that the device would trip out as soon as the circuit was switched on.

Ratings of 5 mA and 10 mA are used in special situations, but the standard rating is 30 mA. This may seem a high shock current, but it must be remembered that RCDs will usually trip within 40 ms (forty thousandths of a second), so that although they do not prevent shock, they will ensure that it is effective for only a short time and is not lethal.

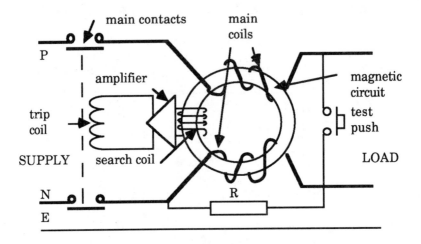

Figure 6.7   Residual current device (circuit breaker)

It must be appreciated that the RCD is only useful as a second line of defence and must not be used as the only protection against electric shock. Correct operation must also be frequently tested using the built-in test facility described above.

There are situations where more than one residual current device will be in use. For example, a complete installation may be protected by a device with a 100 mA rating, whilst 30 mA RCDs are used for protection of particular areas, such as sockets intended to feed equipment to be used out of doors. Discrimination of the devices is then important. For example, if an earth fault results in an earth current of 250 mA on a circuit protected by a 30 mA rated device, both this RCD and that rated at 100 mA will become unbalanced. It is important that the lower rated device operates first, so that only the faulty system is disconnected and not the whole installation. This is known as discrimination and is achieved by deliberately building a time-delay (perhaps 150 ms) into the operation of the higher rated RCD.

There are currently four types of RCD:

Class AC types are used where the residual current is sinusoidal - this is the normal type and is most widely used

Class A types are used where the residual current is sinusoidal and/or includes pulsating direct current. This type is applied in special situations where electronic equipment is in use.

Class B is for specialist operation on pure direct current or on impulse direct or alternating current.

Class S types have a built-in time delay to provide discrimination as described above

6.7.9 Double insulation (Regulation 8)

This method of construction is widely used for electric tools. All live parts of the appliance are insulated, and then protected by a further layer of insulation, so that every live part is surrounded by two layers of insulation. Although the appliance concerned may have accessible metal parts (for example, the chuck of an electric drill) there is no need to earth them because of their double insulation. Flexible cords and cables to double insulated appliances contain no earth wire. Double insulated equipment is usually categorised as Class II (*see* Section 8.3.3).

The BS symbol for double insulation is shown in Figure 6.8. Double-insulated appliances must be regularly inspected and tested. Factory built assemblies of double insulated electrical equipment are covered by BS 5486.

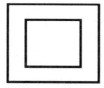

Figure 6.8 British Standard symbol for double insulation

6.8 THE INTEGRITY OF CONDUCTORS AND CONNECTIONS (Regulations 9 and 10)

6.8.1 Referenced conductor integrity (Regulation 9)

The standard method of protecting users of electrical systems against lethal electric shocks is to ensure that the impedance of the fault circuit in the event of an earth fault (the earth fault loop impedance) is low enough to allow enough fault current to flow to operate the protective system (blow the fuse or trip the circuit breaker) before the person can have received a shock for long enough for it to be fatal. These times are specified in the IEE Wiring Regulations (BS 7671) as 5 s for fixed appliance circuits and 0.4 s for socket outlet circuits.

If a connection in this earth fault loop is broken, or if its impedance is increased, the amount of fault current which will flow will not be sufficient to ensure that the protective system cuts off the supply quickly enough to prevent danger. In this connection it is of particular importance that the neutral of the supply should be sound, and should never be lost. Thus, there must be no single pole switches or fuses in the neutral conductor of an installation, particularly because failure of the neutral will prevent normal operation of the circuit, making it appear to be dead and safe. In fact, the dangerously high potential above earth will still be present, as indicated in Figure 6.9. This figure shows the failure of the neutral fuse in a double-pole fused circuit, but exactly the same danger would occur if the circuit were wired with a single-pole switch in the neutral. The neutral may only be switched by one pole of a double-pole switch which is linked so that operation will open the phase (live) and the neutral simultaneously.

6.8.2 Connections (Regulation 10)
It is, perhaps, self evident that connections of the electrical system must be safe and secure. A large number of accidents do occur, however, due to faulty connections, particularly in flexible cords feeding portable appliances.

Perhaps the most obvious rule is to ensure that joints are never made in flexible cords, so that they can never be faulty. There will always be situations where a cord will be extended because it is too short, or where one becomes damaged and is joined after cutting out the faulty part. If such joints are made, they must always be safe, secure and well insulated. But remember, the best precaution is to *never join flexible cords!*

Sometimes it is useful to make use of a properly constructed cable connector, which is correctly and securely connected to the ends of the cord, and which can be plugged together to make the circuit. In such a case, it is important to ensure that such a connector has a protective (earth) connection when one is needed (if the appliance it feeds is not double insulated, for example) and that the side of the connector with male pins is always fixed to the appliance and not to the supply. If the wrong connection is made, the exposed male pins will be live when the connector is pulled apart and the supply is still connected *(see* Figure 6.10)

6.9 LIST OF SHOCK PREVENTION MEASURES

This Chapter has been concerned particularly with the avoidance of the danger of electric shock. The following check list will perhaps prove useful to ensure that all the necessary protective measures have been taken. Make sure that:
1. the polarity of the installation is correct throughout,
2. enclosures and barriers are complete and safe,
3. RCDs are provided wherever necessary, and that a system is in place for their regular testing,
4. protective conductors (earth wires) are large enough to ensure that pro spective fault currents will open the protective system quickly enough,

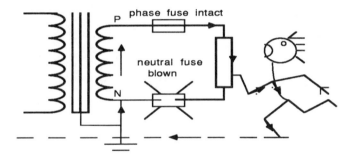

Figure 6.9   Danger from a circuit with a blown fuse in the neutral of a double-pole fused system

5. your electrician has measured the earth fault loop impedance at every outlet (socket and fixed appliance) and ensured that it is equal to or less than the value required by the IEE Wiring Regulations (BS 7671),
6. connections of all protective conductors (earth wires) are mechanically and electrically sound,
7. all electrical insulation is in good condition and is effective,
8. all final circuits are electrically separated from each other (no common neutrals),
9. all portable appliances and tools are regularly inspected and tested, and

10.   where earth-free and non-conducting locations are present they are tested and inspected frequently to ensure that their integrity is secure.

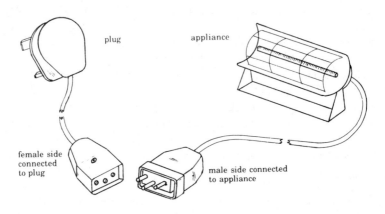

Figure 6.10   Correctly fitted flexible cord connector

Safe Working and Permits-to-Work

7.1 DUTIES OF PERSONS (Regulation 3)

7.1.1 Introduction

The Electricity at Work Regulations 1989 were made under the Health and Safety at Work Act 1974, which imposes duties on the persons using electrical equipment or electrical systems. These duties apply both to the employer and to the employee, and are listed in the two following sections.

7.1.2 An employer's duties (Regulation 3)

The Health and Safety at Work etc Act 1974 specifies in Section 2 the duties of an employer, which are to provide:

1.   a safe working environment,

2.   a safe place of work,

3.   adequate information,

4.   suitable instruction,

5.   skilled supervision where appropriate,

6.   safe methods of handling articles and substances in use,

7.   safe systems of work, and

8.   safe plant, tools and equipment.

7.1.3 An employee's duties (Regulation 3)

It is a requirement in law (Health and Safety at Work *etc* Act 1974 Section 7) that every employee should be responsible for the safety of himself and of others at the place of work. It is worth quoting two sections of the Act in full. They are:

Health and Safety at Work Act
Section 7
It shall be the duty of every employee while at work —
a)   to take reasonable care for the health and safety of himself and of other persons who may be affected by his acts or omissions at work; and
b)   as regards any duty or requirement imposed on his employer or any other person by or under any of the relevant statutory provisions, to co-operate with him so far as is necessary to enable that duty or requirement to be performed or complied with.

This Section of the Act means that the employee must be totally responsible all the time for the safety of the workplace, not only as it affects himself, but also as it affects his fellows. The application of the word "reasonable" was discussed in Chapter 1.

Health and Safety at Work Act
Section 8
No person shall intentionally or recklessly interfere with or misuse anything provided in the interests of health, safety or welfare in pursuance of any relevant statutory provisions.

This Section of the Act makes it clear that employees are required to behave responsibly at all times. A reckless failure to comply with this requirement could conceivably lead to a fatality to another employee and to a prison sentence for the employee at fault.

7.2   WORK ACTIVITIES (Regulation 4)

Regulation 4(3) requires that all work activities shall be carried out in ways which do not give rise to danger. This is a general Regulation which covers the whole range of work which may be carried out, whether electrical or not. For example, an electrical contractor employed to clean and re-lamp high bay luminaires may well start work by erecting a staging to give him the necessary access to the work. This process of erecting a non-electrical structure is subject to the Electricity at Work Regulations, just as much as is the maintenance of a high-voltage switchboard.

The duty of workers to comply with the Regulations applies to all work activities without exception, and includes work close to an electrical system from which danger could arise. For example, if the staging for access to lighting is erected close to an open electrical switchboard, danger will occur if it topples over onto the live system. If this is possible, precautions must be taken to prevent danger, one conceivable action being to switch off the supply to the switchboard.

The Regulation must be followed so far as is reasonably practical. In other words, if the person responsible for work on the lighting felt that it was not reasonable to switch off the supply to the open switchboard (and perhaps to prevent work activities continuing over a wide area), he takes the responsibility for the action and may be required to justify it at a court hearing if an accident takes place.

7.3 PROVISION OF PROTECTIVE EQUIPMENT (Regulation 4)

This Regulation requires that equipment provided to protect those working on or near electrical equipment must be suitable for its intended use, must be maintained in good condition and must be properly used.

7.3.1 Suitability (Regulation 4)
Where an employee provides his own tools or protective equipment, as required by his conditions of employment, he has responsibilities for his working practices as covered by Regulation 4(3) (*see* Section 7.2). In these cases it is the duty of the employer to make sure that:
1. he has specified the right tools and equipment to be provided by the employee, and
2. he checks frequently to ensure that the employee has provided suitable tools and equipment, maintains them in good condition and uses them properly and safely.

7.3.2 Protective equipment   (Regulation 4)
Special equipment is often needed to ensure the safety of those working on electrical systems, and must always be provided when required. This Regulation is not qualified by the words "as far as is reasonably practical", so

safety equipment must always be provided when it is necessary. In every case, safety equipment must meet three requirements, which are:

1. Suitable for use
All safety equipment must be manufactured to recognised British Standards, although in the case of test instruments, Continental standards such as the German VDE specifications, are often used and are acceptable. In every case, the employer must make a proper analysis of the tasks which will need safety equipment, what items must be provided and how such devices will be used.

2. Properly maintained
Safety equipment which is not regularly tested and inspected will necessarily depreciate as it becomes older. For example, the insulated handle of a screwdriver may crack if not carefully treated, so that the safety it is expected to provide will be lost in use. A proper system of inspection and testing of safety equipment is a requirement for any well-run organisation. It should be possible to consult records to discover at any time when a particular piece of equipment was last inspected and tested, together with the results of those tests where this is applicable. This will apply to all equipment used, such as rubber gloves, rubber mats, enclosures, electrical test instruments, and so on. In the case of test instruments, periodic recalibration is necessary to ensure that the readings provided can be relied upon and records maintained giving details of the calibrations.

3. Properly used
Whilst the employee is likely to be directly involved in using the safety equipment, it is the duty of the employer to see that it is used safely and correctly. In this respect, the employer must ensure that those under his command have been properly trained and are well supervised to ensure that they follow safe working practices.

7.4 CUTTING OFF ELECTRICAL SUPPLIES
(Regulation 12)
7.4.1 Introduction
If an electrical system is to be made safe for work, it is, perhaps, obvious

that the electrical supply to it should be switched off. It is not always obvious where the switch for a particular circuit or equipment will be found, and thus careful and correct identification of switches becomes necessary. As well as switching off, the person working on the system will want to be sure that the supply is not restored whilst he is at work. Thus, there must also be a system of isolation. There are thus two separate and distinct requirements:

1.   cutting off the supply, and
2.   isolation

7.4.2   Cutting off the supply (Regulation 12)

Every electrical installation will have a mains position, where there will be switches which can be used to cut off the supply to the part of the installation on which work is required. In the case of a small installation, it is possible that there will be only one switch which controls all the electrical circuits. In such a case, it may be necessary to cut off the supply to the required circuit by removal of the circuit fuse or by operation of the circuit breaker concerned.

In a larger installation, the switch required may not be at the mains position, but in a sub-main board. Again, in some circumstances it may be necessary to withdraw a fuse or to switch off a circuit breaker to effect removal of the supply. In all cases, the main switchgear must be accessible for operation and maintenance, but must also be secured against unauthorised operation. The switching system must be common to several parts of an electrical installation only where it is appropriate for all those parts to be switched as a group.

Whether the system is small or large, there is a clear need for careful identification of the means of switching off. The person concerned must be quite sure that the correct circuit has been made dead, and he can only be sure of this if all switches, fuses and circuit breakers are identified clearly in terms of the systems they feed. In the case of a large installation, it may become necessary to consult circuit or schematic diagrams to identify the correct fuse or switch. If this is so, then such diagrams must be readily available to the person concerned, usually at the mains or sub-mains position.

7.4.3 Isolation (Regulation 12)

It would be foolhardy of a worker to assume that because he has removed a certain fuse or switched off a circuit breaker, that the circuit concerned is dead and safe to work on. In some cases he will need to test the circuit to ensure that it is dead, and/or he may be able to be certain of safety by isolating it. In fact, isolation is always a requirement, in addition to switching off. In some cases a special isolator will be provided, but in others the worker will need to isolate by removing circuit connections. Requirements for isolators are that they must:

1. ensure a definite break of all live conductors,
2. be designed to prevent inadvertent reclosing,
3. have definite indication of their present state, *i.e.* open or closed,
4. have adequate clearance between contacts to ensure that current can not flow between them, for example, by surface leakage,
5. be located in positions readily available to those who need to use them,
6. be arranged to prevent unauthorised operation, for example by pro vision of locking-off facilities,
7. isolate only the system required to be dead, unless it is usual to re move the supply simultaneously from a group of circuits,
8. be clearly labelled to indicate the systems that they control, and
9. have means for isolating control circuits where remote operation is employed.

If the isolator is in the form of a switch, it is not required to be capable of cutting off circuit current, but simply to prevent the circuit from being re-energised when it is switched off. If isolation is by removal of a fuse, it is important to first switch off the load(s) to prevent dangerous arcing at the fuse.

7.5 SAFE WORKING SYSTEMS (Regulation 13)

7.5.1 Working dead (Regulation 13)

Obviously this is the preferred method of working on an electrical system. The dead circuit(s) must be incapable of causing harm, but to ensure that a system is dead and safe to work on is often a more complicated procedure than it would seem. First of all, it must never be assumed that a circuit or system is dead until it has been proved to be so. The full procedure, which it is sometimes sensible to abbreviate, is:

1. Switch off
Switch off the supply to the circuit (*see* 7.4.2)

2. Isolate
This may be by operation of an isolating switch, or may be by disconnection of the circuit supply cables (*see* 7.4.3)

3. Post warning notices
Two forms of notice are involved. Firstly, isolating switches must have notices affixed to warn that they must under no circumstances be reclosed. Secondly, the approaches to the site of the work must have notices displayed to make it clear to anyone arriving that they must stay away from the work being carried out. In view of the fact that warning notices have been provided on the isolators (*see* 2. above) it may seem to be 'overkill' to also lock them off. However, we must remember that there will always be those who ignore notices, or perhaps they are unable to read them.

4. Lock off
The object here is so that the person who is in contact with the circuit is confident that it is impossible for it to be made live without his knowledge. If he has disconnected cables close to where the work is taking place, he can see that they are not reconnected. If an isolating switch is out of his sight, there must be provision for locking it off, for example using a padlock to hold the operating handle in the OFF position to which he keeps the key. Another method is to make the operating handle removable in the OFF position so he can take it with him.

5. Test
No circuit must ever be assumed to be dead and safe until it has been proved to be so. The standard method is to use a voltmeter to measure the potential difference between the circuit concerned and earth. In this case the voltmeter must be tested before operation (ideally by measurements on the circuit concerned before it is switched off) and again afterwards.

6. Earth

Some circuits may become charged during operation, so that severe shocks from them are possible even after switching off. This effect is most common where capacitors are connected, for example for power factor correction. The circuits should be securely connected to earth to ensure that no potential difference is possible from the conductors to the general mass of earth. This precaution is especially effective for outdoor working, when an unexpected lightning strike could charge the working circuit.

7. Issue permit to work

This requirement is usually only for special circumstances, where unusually complex circuitry or high voltages are concerned. It will be fully considered in Section 7.6.

On completion of the work, the safety precautions listed above should be removed in reverse order once the responsible person is satisfied that it is safe to do so.

Useful guidance on the safe operation and maintenance of switchgear and distribution systems will be found in HSE OP 10, BS 6423, BS 6626 and BS 6867.

7.5.2 Live working (Regulation 14)

Live working on any electrical system (which is not made safe by suitable insulation) is not permitted by the Electricity at Work Regulations 1989 unless:

1.   it is unreasonable in all the circumstances for the the system to be dead, and
2.   it is reasonable in all the circumstances for work to be carried out whilst the system is live, and
3.   suitable precautions (including the provision of suitable protective equipment where necessary) are taken to prevent injury.

Regulation 14 makes it clear that there must never be live working unless there is absolutely no way of avoiding it. In this respect, it should be pointed out that inconvenience to others due to the loss of their electrical supply is unlikely to be a satisfactory defence in the event of a legal action following an accident.

Where live working really is unavoidable, proper precautions must be taken to avoid accidents and injury, and it will be up to the employer to justify the decision to work live and to demonstrate that all possible precautions were taken. If all the necessary safety precautions cannot be taken, there will be no option but to switch off the supply and to work on a dead system. The employer must assess the risk and take precautions which will depend on the level of risk. If he feels that he does not have the knowledge and experience to judge the case, he should seek the advice of a competent person.

Live working is a specialised field, which should not be entered by those not fully trained and totally conversant with the dangers. When live working is carried out, the following precautions should be observed:

1. only fully trained and competent persons must be involved,

2. they must be provided with suitable equipment, protective clothing and insulated tools which have been recently tested,

3. they must be fully provided with information concerning the task being performed and the system on which they are working,

4. suitable insulating screens and barriers must be provided where appropriate,

5. suitable and adequate test equipment must be provided, together with suitable probes for connection to live equipment without danger to the user,

6. it may be helpful to provide notices which give details of emergency resuscitation in situations where live working is taking place. Suitably trained first aiders, ideally those engaged on the work itself, should also be available,

7. the area round the working space must be properly controlled to prevent the entry of unauthorised persons or animals, and

8. consideration must be given to the possible need for a single worker to be accompanied by a competent colleague so that prompt assistance is available in the event of an accident.

It cannot be stressed too strongly that live working should never be undertaken unless absolutely necessary, and then only by those trained and competent to carry it out. In most cases it is important that a person working on a live electrical system should be accompanied by at least one other, who will be able to apply rescue and resuscitation techniques or to call for help in the event of an accident.

Statistics show that a high proportion of accidents with live systems are amongst those who had no intention of working on live systems, notably those who inadvertently make contact with live underground or overhead cables. These workers come within the scope of Regulation 14, and are usually concerned with excavations in the vicinity of underground cables, working from platforms, scaffolding or roofs or with movement of high vehicles (cranes, agricultural machinery, and so on) near overhead lines.

Excavation workers are particularly at risk when using hand tools such as pick axes and concrete breakers, and precautions should include:

1.   mapping and recording the site of all underground cable runs,

2.   providing suitable cable marking tape or cable tiles above the cable,

3.   using cable location devices before starting to excavate, and

4.   employing digging practices which are known to be safe.

Those who may be in danger from overhead lines should follow the guidance given in Health and Safety Executive guidance note GS 6, "Avoidance of danger from overhead electric lines". This is particularly the case in agricultural and horticultural situations.

7.6   THE PERMIT-TO-WORK SYSTEM (Regulation 14)
7.6.1   Principle
The permit-to-work is a well-tried safety measure which is widely used where danger is possible when working on electrical systems. Its basis is that we are all much more careful of our actions when we know that there can be no doubt that we will carry the blame for what we have done if things go wrong.

To this end, rules apply in many situations which make it clear that no work must be started until the person in charge of those who will carry it out is in possession of a valid permit-to-work. The permit is issued by a suitably qualified engineer, who holds the authority to issue permits, and who first makes the work safe by following the steps specified in 7.5.1 (switch off, isolate, post warning notices, lock off, test, earth) and then completes the permit. This is in duplicate, the top copy being given to the person in charge of the actual work, who signs the copy to accept responsibility for the specified work and to confirm that no attempt will be made to work on systems not covered by the permit.

He keeps the permit whilst the work is carried out, and then returns it to the responsible person, having confirmed with his signature on the copy that the work is complete and that others in his charge have been warned that they may no longer safely work on the installation in question. The responsible person then signs the copy to cancel the permit, before removing earth connections, locks and notices and then restores the supply. All signatures are timed and dated. The original of the permit is destroyed after the work has been completed, but the copy is retained, usually in a permit-to-work book.

Should an accident happen, it is possible to see clearly from the book copy of the permit who was at fault. For example, if the responsible person fails to lock an isolator, which is reclosed to cause the accident, the fault is clearly his. Alternatively, if the person in charge of the operations carries out, or orders those working for him to carry out, work on a system not covered by the permit, he is at fault.

It will sound as if the object is to apportion blame after an accident. In fact, the presence of the system makes accidents unlikely because those at work know that if an accident occurs the person who has acted wrongly may be held responsible. Under these circumstances, people will take greater care to follow the rules precisely.

7.6.2 Sample Permit-to-Work

There are many versions of the permit-to-work produced to suit differing situations and circumstances. There is no objection to this provided that they follow the principles laid down in the previous section. The sample permit which follows is intended to help the reader to understand the principle, and will not necessarily be suitable in a particular case.

PERMIT-TO-WORK (FRONT)

Serial number

Issued to ....in charge of the work

I hearby declare that the following apparatus is dead, isolated from all live conductors and is connected to earth.

The system is isolated at the following points:

Caution notices have been posted at :

Safety locks have been fitted at :

The work to be carried out is:

Diagram

Signed by (Name in block capitals)

Signed .... Time ....Date............

Receipt

I accept responsibility for carrying out the work on the system detailed in this permit-to-work and no attempt will be made by me or persons under my control to work on other systems

Signed by (Name in block capitals)

Signed .... Time ....Date............

PERMIT-TO-WORK (BACK)

Clearance
The work for which this permit was issued is now completed/suspended*
and all persons under my charge have been withdrawn and warned that it is
no longer safe to work on the system covered by this permit.

The work is complete/incomplete*

All gear and tools have/have not* been removed

Additional earths have/have not* been removed

* delete the words not applicable, and where necessary state:

Abnormalities are at

Additional earths are at

Signed by (Name in block capitals)

Signed .... Time ....Date ....

Cancellation
This permit to work is cancelled

Signed by (Name in block capitals)

Signed .... Time ....Date ....

8
Portable Appliances

8.1 INTRODUCTION

Perhaps it seems strange that a complete Chapter should be devoted to the subject of portable appliances. However, it has been shown that more than 25% of electrical accidents at work involve portable electrical appliances. It follows that an employer must take special care to ensure that users of such appliances are protected from electric shock and fire hazards. The same requirements must also apply when clients use the appliances in shops, hospitals, hotels and so on, as well as those who rent, repair or re-sell such appliances.

It is important to appreciate that as far as the Electricity at Work Regulations are concerned, ALL portable appliances are covered. Thus they embrace not only those often considered to be hazardous, such as drills, grinders, *etc.*, but also all those other every-day appliances that are so often taken for granted, such as floor polishers, kettles, coffee makers, computers, desk lamps and so on. Any appliance fed from a plug and socket of any kind is covered. Those appliances which are hand-held in use are clearly more likely to pose danger to the user than others which are portable but not in such close contact with the user during operation. It is prudent to inspect and test such appliances more frequently than is necessary for other types. Some appliances are too heavy or too cumbersome to be moved frequently, but are never-the-less supplied from plugs and sockets. Such appliances are called transportable appliances.

Portable appliances for use in the fields of aerospace, medicine, marine situations, diving and welding are likely to need special testing and inspection.

A properly organised and planned programme of inspection and testing of all portable appliances is thus necessary to meet the requirements of the Electricity at Work Regulations 1989. The system introduced to deal with portable appliances should ensure that:

1.   the testing of appliances is the special responsibility of particular members of staff,

2.   a register of all appliances is kept, arranged so that all equipment is inspected and tested at the required intervals, and

3.   all appliances are labelled to show the date of the last and of the next inspection and test.

8.2 INSPECTION   (Regulations 4.2, 10)

Although testing will reveal many of the possible hazards of using appliances, it will often not show up dangers arising as a result of damage to supply leads, plugs, and so on. A part of the regular maintenance procedure must be to inspect every piece of portable equipment. The inspector must look for:

1.   whether the equipment is suitable for its environment. For example, a piece of equipment which will be used out of doors must be of waterproof construction (IPX3),

2.   whether the equipment is suitable for the work it is required to do. For example, a small hand drill intended for domestic use is unlikely to be satisfactory when used continuously on a construction site,

3.   excessive use of trailing socket outlets or multiway adaptors,

4.   unprotected cables and flexible cords run under carpets. Ideally, flexible cords should be visible throughout their length,

5.   damaged flexible cords resulting in live cables being exposed to touch,

6.   badly made joints in flexible cords with exposed circuit or protective conductors, or which subject the conductors to undue strain,

7.   the use of extension leads which are unnecessarily long; if equipment cannot be fed except by the use of such leads, consideration should be given to the provision of a local socket outlet. If extension leads are necessary, they should be inspected and tested as Class I equipment to comply with the HSE requirements. Extension leads should never be longer than 12 m if the core area is 1.25 mm^2, 15 m if 1.5 mm^2, or 25 m if 2.5 mm^2. Note that 2.5 mm^2 flexible cord is too large to be connected to a BS 1363 13 A plug, but may be connected to a BS 4343 industrial plug. In the event of extension leads being unavoidably longer than these lengths, the lead and

the appliance it feeds should be protected with an RCD of rating not exceeding 30 mA,

8.   damage to flexible cords resulting in the failure of the protective conductor (earth wire),

9.   the fuse tightness in the plug,

10.   the correct fuse size. British Standards only recognise 3 A and 13 A fuses, corresponding to maximum loads of 700 W and 3 kW respectively. However, several manufacturers also provide fuses rated at 2 A (450 W), 5 A (1150 W) and 10 A (2.3 kW),

11.   cables in positions where damage may result from their being trodden on or snagged,

12.   a missing cover or damage to the plug so that unsheathed conductors are exposed or broken,

13.   damage to the appliance so that unsheathed conductors are exposed or broken,

14.   failure of the cord grip at the plug or at the appliance so that insulated but unsheathed cables are exposed, or so that conductors are in danger of being pulled from their terminals,

15.   failure of the cord grip at the plug or at the appliance so that undue strain is applied to the terminals when the cord is pulled,

16.   wrong connections in the plug or at the appliance. The fact that an appliance appears to be working correctly is not proof that the connections are correctly made. Incorrect connections may possibly cause danger in the event of a fault,

17.   other visible damage which could possibly result in an accident, such as damage to the casing, loose or missing screws, *etc.*,

18.   equipment which is not properly ventilated because it is too close to a wall or because ventilation apertures are blocked,

19.   everyday items placed dangerously, for example plants or cups, which may be tipped over so that soil or liquid enters the equipment,

20.   a readily available means of disconnection (note that damage to equipment or loss of data may result if business equipment is disconnected without following the correct procedure),

21.   obvious physical damage to the equipment, its lead or its plug,

22.   signs of overheating of the equipment, its lead or its plug,

23.   signs of the ingress of foreign materials, such as liquids, and
24.   signs of fire damage.

The revised edition of the HSE Guidance Note PM32 particularly warns of the special hazards posed by the build-up of dust within an appliance. Where it is known that dust may accumulate within an appliance, the periodic inspection may need to include dismantling and internal cleaning.

It is important that this visual inspection is carried out before tests are made. There are circumstances where the tester will be in danger if a faulty appliance is tested, particularly where live conductors are exposed. The inspection will, in most cases, show up the results of normal "wear and tear" on an appliance. If equipment is found to be faulty or damaged on inspection or test, a responsible person must make an assessment as to the suitability of the item for the work it is doing and for the location in which it is used. If the equipment is unsuitable, frequent inspections and tests will not make it suitable, and replacement is necessary. In particularly difficult or dirty situations, the need for more frequent inspection and test should be considered.

Care is necessary when dealing with equipments which have optical fibre connections. Such a cable may be disconnected from the appliance whilst still leaving the laser drive in place. In such a case, eye damage may result if a person looks directly into the end of a cable or a connector.

8.3 TESTING (Regulations 4.2, 10)

8.3.1 Introduction

The requirement to test appliances regularly and to file the results of such tests applies to all employers of people who use electrical appliances in the course of their work. Since special test equipment and expertise is often needed, the smaller firm may well put such work out for completion by an outside contractor. It must be stressed that the requirement for periodic inspection and testing applies to all who use portable electrical equipment at work, not only to larger employers.

A type of fault which has always been difficult to rectify is one which is intermittent in nature. Almost invariably it is not present during testing, but appears again immediately the appliance concerned is put back into service. In this connection, a multimeter has now become available which will capture an intermittent voltage or continuity irregularity, thus proving its presence and making fault rectification easier.

8.3.2 What and when?

The question arises as to what appliances are covered by the inspection and testing requirements. In many cases employers think of it as covering power tools only. This is not correct. Any appliance which may be plugged into a socket (13 A type to BS 1363, and industrial types to BS 196 and BS 4343) is included and must be inspected and tested. As well as power tools, the list includes electrical radiant and convector heaters, kettles, typewriters, computers and printers, desk lamps, coffee machines, floor polishers, *etc*.

110 V tools for use in industrial situations are, of course, also included.

There are four sets of circumstances in which safety testing of appliances becomes imperative. These are where:

1.   employees are using, or are likely to use, the organisation's portable appliances,

2.   electrical appliances are sold or hired. In the latter case, inspection and testing should be carried out after each hiring and before the appliance is re-hired,

3.   customers, or other non-employees, are likely to use portable appliances owned by the organisation, and

4.   a repair has been carried out on the appliance. The inspection and test should be completed after repair and before re-use.

Portable equipment is defined as intended to be moved while in operation or while still plugged in to the supply. Transportable equipment (sometimes called movable equipment) is defined as 18 kg or less in mass and not fixed, or on wheels, castors or other means to allow it to be moved by the operator.

Table 8.1 Suggested intervals between inspection and testing of portable appliances

Inspection should be carried out by the user or by a competent person and testing by a competent person

Type of premises	Type of equipment	Frequency of inspection	Frequency of testing
Industrial	hand-held	before use	6 months
	portable	before use	12 months
	transportable	before use	12 months
	business equip.	before use	12 months
Construction	hand-held	before use	3 months
	portable	before use	3 months
	transportable	before use	3 months
Equipment hire	hand-held	before use	before issue
	portable	before use	before issue
	transportable	before use	before issue
Schools	hand-held	weekly	12 months
	portable	1 month	12 months
	transportable	6 months	12 months
Hotels, halls *etc.*	hand-held	daily	12 months
	portable	daily	12 months
	transportable	daily	12 months
Offices	hand-held	3 months	12 months
	portable	6 months	12 months
	transportable	6 months	12 months
	business equip.	6 months	12 months

An obvious question is "How often should we inspect and test appliances?" There is no direct answer to the question, since the frequency of testing must depend on the type of appliance concerned, the situation in which it is used, the skill of those using it and the frequency of use. Table 8.1 makes some suggestions of intervals between inspections and tests, but the responsible person must use his judgement to reduce the periods as circumstances dictate. It must be appreciated that proper inspection and testing will not in itself result in compliance with the law. Inspection and testing is simply a means of making sure that the equipment concerned will not present danger to its users.

8.3.3 Electrical safety

Two lines of defence are used to prevent the user of a portable appliance from becoming part of an electrical circuit and receiving an electric shock. They are insulation and earthing.

Insulation

The purpose of the insulation is to surround live electrical parts so that the appliance user cannot come into contact with them. It must have very high resistance at the voltage used in the circuit concerned. Inspection will often reveal damaged or worn insulation, but a test of the insulation of apparently sound cables and appliances is still required. The test is carried out between both live connections (the phase (sometimes called the live) and neutral) connected together and the earthing system. Care must be taken if applying an insulation test between live conductors (phase and neutral) since some types of equipment may be damaged as a result. More extensive consideration of insulation testing will be found in Section 8.3.5.

Earthing

The exposed conductive parts of the appliance are connected to earth so that in the event of their becoming live due to a fault, current will flow to earth. The impedance of the circuit must be low so that a high current flows to open the circuit quickly. The IEE Wiring Regulations (BS 7671) require that in the event of an earth fault, a circuit feeding socket outlets should be disconnected by its protection (fuse or circuit breaker) within 0.4 s, as opposed to fixed appliances which may take up to 5 s to disconnect. This is because of the likelihood that the user of a portable appliance, which will be fed from a socket outlet, will be in better contact with it because he will probably grasp it more tightly than would be the case with a fixed appliance.

One method of ensuring the integrity of the earthing system is the use of a monitoring system such as that shown in Fig 8.1. An additional core (the pilot wire) is needed in the flexible cable or cord feeding the appliance, which forms a closed circuit with the earth connection feeding a relay. In the event of a failure of the earthing system, the feed to the relay coil is broken and the supply to the appliance is switched off.

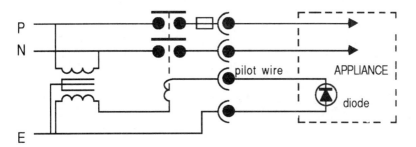

Fig 8.1 Earth monitoring system

There are two types of protection for the user of portable appliances. Safety tests, as we shall see, differ depending on the class of protection provided

Class I protection
This method uses insulation plus earthing, so that the metal case of every Class I portable appliance must be earthed.

Class II protection
This method uses double insulation and appliances are not earthed (see Section 6.7.9). This means that the flexible cords of such appliances will have only two cores (the phase (often called the live) and the neutral) with no earth wire. Class II appliances may have accessible metal, such as a steel casing, but require no earthing. The identification mark for Class II equipment is shown in Figure 8.2.

It is important to appreciate that uninterruptible power supplies (UPS) are designed to maintain the supply, usually from a battery-driven circuit, when the mains supply is lost, so care must be taken to ensure that a piece of equipment is not still live even when unplugged or disconnected. It perhaps goes without saying that a UPS will only be used when it is important that the supply is maintained, so it is vital to check that no damage will result (for example, the loss of data) if an equipment is unplugged or disconnected for test purposes.

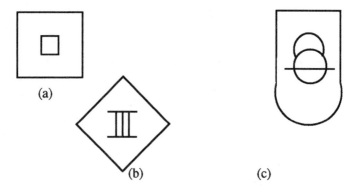

Figure 8.2 Construction marks for:-
                    (a) Class II equipment
                    (b) Class III equipment
                    (c) safety isolating transformer

Class III protection
Class III equipment offers safety to its users because it is a separated extra-low voltage (SELV) system (previously called a safety extra-low voltage system). It involves using equipment fed at not more than 50 V (in most cases at 12 V or 24 V) fed from a safety isolating transformer to BS 3535. Figure 8.2 shows the construction marks for Class III equipments and for safety isolating transformers.

8.3.4 Required tests
When inspection of an appliance is completed, testing will be the next step.

It goes without saying that instruments must be safe, and they will be safe if they comply with BS EN 61010 or with BS 5458. It is particularly important that test leads and probes used to apply or to measure voltages exceeding 50 V a.c. or 100 V d.c. should comply. All test instruments should have their accuracy verified each year by undergoing the process of calibration. There will be three steps for each test, which are:

1.   Earth continuity tests. These must be carried out with a test instrument which provides a high current, so that it will reveal faults such as a partially severed conductor, a loose connection, and so on. This is the Type A test which involves providing a current of 25 A for not less than 3 s from a source of voltage not exceeding 12 V. It should be noted that certain types of electronic business equipment may be damaged by a high-current earth continuity test and must be subjected only to a Type B test, which uses a current not exceeding 200 mA at a voltage not less than 100 mV and not exceeding 24V. Maximum values of earth continuity measured from the earth pin of the plug to the earthed parts of the appliance are shown in Table 8.2, where R is the resistance of the lead. Lead resistances can be calculated from the data given in Table 8.4.

2.   High voltage insulation test applied for not less than 6 s. Care should be taken because, if the voltage is too low, possible problems of insulation breakdown will not be detected, but a high voltage will often destroy electronic components,

3.   Record and date the test results, so that comparison can be made at the next test to reveal any degradation which has occurred.

8.3.5 The portable appliance tester

These devices are commonly called PATs. A wide variety of portable appliance testers is available from a number of manufacturers. The simplest (and the cheapest) of them will simply carry out the basic earthing and insulation tests. More complicated testers will also carry out fuse tests, flash tests, load tests, operation tests and earth leakage tests. Some have a microprocessor facility which enables them to store the results for later print-out via a computer, in which case they are likely to be provided with a keyboard or some other method of identification for the test instrument of the appliance being tested. In some cases a bar code reader is included, allowing the appliance to be labelled distinctively.

Some testers provide their results in analogue (a needle moving over a scale) or in digital form, whilst others simply indicate pass or fail (the "go, no-go" type).

Whatever the type of tester used, it is important that it should be recalibrated periodically to ensure that the results provided are accurate and can be relied upon. Before starting a test, the person carrying out the test must ensure that the appliance is switched on and that its fuse is intact, or any results obtained may be invalid. The tests are usually carried out by plugging the appliance into a socket outlet on the PAT. For some tests, contact is made to the casing of the appliance with an auxiliary probe.

It must be stressed that the PAT is simply a convenient device to facilitate the testing of appliances and equipments. There is no requirement for one to be used, and all the required readings can be carried out by a competent electrician using his normal test instruments.

Having said that, the very large number of tests required, and the high cost of performing them using qualified electricians, has led to widespread use of special portable appliance testers (PATs). Although such testers are very expensive, they do allow testing to be carried out by semi-skilled people, so that the end cost may well be lower. The ability of many of these devices to store results for later downloading to a computer and the ability of many types to read bar codes for appliance identification are added advantages.

There are two main tests.

Earth test   (often called the earth bond test)

The auxiliary probe is connected to the exposed metalwork casing and the appliance plugged in to the PAT. A heavy current, typically 25 A, is passed through the earthing system for not less than 3 s, and the tester calculates and indicates the resistance of the earthing system. The high current will show up a fault such as a loose connection or a partially severed conductor. This test is not required in the case of double insulated (class II) devices.

Some types of business equipment are unusual in that some exposed conductive parts may not be earthed for reasons of electromagnetic compatibility (EMC). In these cases, usually computer-based equipments such as cash tills and so on, earthing the parts may result in an induced EMF which will adversely affect the working of the system. If a high current test is applied in these circumstances, the equipment may suffer damage.

The pass level for this test is usually 0.1 Ω, although for some types of electronic equipment values of up to 0.5 Ω may be acceptable. If very long cables are in use, the result will be higher, and it will become necessary to calculate the resistance of the earth wire, or to obtain it from the cable manufacturer, to assess the test result. Table 8.4 gives the resistances of standard sizes of conductors in flexible cords for three usual lengths, expressed in Ω (ohms).

Table 8.2 Maximum earth continuity for appliances

Equipment	Maximum resistance
household appliances	$(0.1 + R)\,\Omega$
luminaires	$0.5\,\Omega$ (inc. supply cable)
electronic apparatus	$(0.5 + R)\,\Omega$
motor operated tools	$(0.1 + R)\,\Omega$
information technology equipment	$(0.1 + R)\,\Omega$

R is the resistance of the appliance lead

Insulation test

A voltage of 500 V DC is applied between the current-carrying conductors (which are connected together for the duration of the test) and earth for not less than 6 s. It is often convenient to provide a special test socket with phase and neutral permanently connected into which the appliance is plugged during the insulation test. There is then less chance of the temporary connections being left in place after the test. Double insulated (class II) appliances have no earth, so the test is from each of the current-carrying conductors to the metal case if there is one, or to a clip held against the appliance body during the test for insulated case appliances The minimum accept able values of earth continuity resistance are given in Table 8.3 for Class I and for Class II appliances. Different values apply when the equipment is new and when it has been in service.

Table 8.3 Minimum insulation resistance for appliances

Equipment	Class I appliance		Class II appliance	
	As new	In service	As new	In service
household appliances	2 MΩ	0.5 MΩ	7 MΩ	1 MΩ
luminaires	2 MΩ	0.5 MΩ	4 MΩ	1 MΩ
electronic apparatus	2 MΩ	0.5 MΩ	4 MΩ	1 MΩ
motor op. tools	2 MΩ	0.5 MΩ	7 MΩ	1 MΩ
info tech equip.	2 MΩ	0.5 MΩ	2 MΩ	1 MΩ

Table 8.4 Resistance of flexible cords in ohms					
Flexible cord	*cross-sectional area (mm²)*				
length (m)	*0.5*	*0.75*	*1.0*	*1.25*	*1.5*
1.0	0.040	0.027	0.020	0.016	0.014
2.0	0.079	0.054	0.040	0.032	0.027
3.0	0.119	0.080	0.059	0.048	0.041
4.0	0.158	0.105	0.079	0.064	0.054
5.0	0.197	0.132	0.098	0.080	0.067

Care must be taken with some types of equipment to ensure that components connected between live conductors and earth (such as those in filter networks) are disconnected if their ratings are such that they would suffer damage from the test voltage. It is important to ensure that the tester used really does provide the required level of voltage. There is a number of inferior testers available which will provide 500 V on open circuit, but which are unable to sustain this voltage level even when applied to high levels of insulation resistance.

In some cases the application of the high voltage required for the insulation test will cause damage to the equipment under test. Where this seems possible, the supplier must be consulted to verify the position. Where damage could result, the earth leakage method or the touch current measurement method must be used. To apply this method, the rated supply voltage is applied between phase and neutral connected together and the earth system. The current in the circuit is measured using a low-reading milliammeter. The insulation resistance is then calculated by application of Ohm's law:

$$R = \frac{V}{I}$$

where R is the insulation resistance of the equipment under test,
V is the applied direct voltage,
I is the measured leakage current,

Calculation will show that the leakage current for a healthy equipment will be very low indeed. For example, if 230 V is applied to an insulation resistance of 1 M the leakage current will be 0.23 mA.

If the equipment is new and is being tested before being put into service, the required test voltage must be 1.06 times the rated voltage. Thus, for a 230 V rated appliance, the applied test voltage must be 244 V. The leakage current must be measured within 5 s after the application of the test voltage.

Table 8.5 Maximum Permissible Leakage Currents
(taken from BS 3456, BS 4533 and BS 5784)

Type of Appliance	Max. Leakage Current
Household appliances (BS3456)	
Portable Class I	0.75 mA
Stationary Class I motor-operated	3.5 mA
Stationary Class I heaters	0.75 mA/kW
	5 mA max for appliance
All Class II	0.25 mA
Commercial catering appliances (BS 5784)	
Portable Class I motor-operated	0.75 mA/kW with 3.5 mA max.
Stationary Class I heaters	1.0 mA/kW
	10 mA max for appliance fed via a plug but no max. when fixed
Class II	0.25 mA
Luminaires (BS 4533)	
Class I portable or fixed	1.0 mA to 1 kVA
Class I fixed over 1 kVA	1.0 mA/kVA up to 5 mA
Class II	0.5 mA

In addition to these two main tests, there is a series of other tests which are desirable to ensure safety.

Touch current measurement

This test is used as an alternative to insulation resistance measurement where either the insulation test cannot be carried out or where there are concerns that such a test may damage equipment. The test is available as an option on many PAT testers, which will indicate if the value measured is acceptable. Touch current is the current that flows through the body when a person in contact with the general mass of earth touches accessible parts of equipment, usually Class II (which have no earth connection and hence no path for protective current) and should be very low, typically 0.25mA. In the event of the protective conductor of a Class I appliance breaking or becoming disconnected, the protective current becomes the touch current. This is why protective currents in Class I appliances are limited to 3.5 mA.

Fuse test

This continuity test confirms that the fuse is intact and that the appliance is switched on prior to other tests.

Flash test

This is a higher-voltage test than the insulation test, and is carried out at 1.5 kV for class 1 and at 3 kV for class 2 appliances. The test voltage is alternating (AC) applied for not less than 6 s so that capacitance effects are included, and leakage current is measured. If there is an automatic indication of breakdown which can be reset by the operator the time of application may be reduced to 2 s. For a pass level, leakage current should typically be below 3 mA *(see* Table 8.5 for more detail). The remarks concerning the vulnerability of certain types of component made under insulation testing will also apply to this type of test.

Flash tests should not be carried out on electronic equipment which may be damaged by the high voltages involved. Flash testing is not likely to be required except after equipment repair.

Load test

This test measures the resistance of the appliance to the current flow through it, and thus confirms that it is not too low for safe operation. A low load test resistance would indicate that the appliance will take more current than normal when connected. There may be a need to consult manufacturers in cases where the appliance contains its own power source (such as batteries) or where devices with variable resistance components, such as fluorescent lamps, are present.

It is important to appreciate that the test cannot be used for appliances which include motors. In these cases, the actual resistance of the motor may be very low and will indicate that current will be excessive, but a voltage developed in the motor when it is running which opposes the supply voltage (sometimes called "back EMF") limits the amount of current flowing.

The pass level can be calculated from the voltage and current ratings of the device, although special factors may need to be considered where equipments with a power factor other than unity are concerned.

$$R = \frac{V}{I} \text{ or } R = \frac{V^2}{P}$$

where R is the normal resistance of the appliance ( ),
      V is the nominal supply voltage (V) at normal frequency,
      I   is the nominal appliance current (A) and
      P is the power rating of the appliance (W) assuming unity power factor.

Manufacturers will advise a course of action where there is doubt.

Operation test
This is a further test of the current carried during normal operation to check that the current drawn is not excessive. This test simply verifies the effectiveness of the load test.

Earth leakage test
This test is normally applied only to single insulated (class I) appliances, because double insulated (class II) have no earth connection to which leakage current will flow. However, it can be applied to class II appliances which are tightly wrapped in a conducting foil to which leakage will occur. Leakage current for SELV (separated extra-low voltage) appliances may also need to be measured in some cases.

The test measures the leakage current to earth during normal operation. It is useful in that an increasing level of leakage current from one test to the next indicates a deterioration in the appliance insulation. Another advantage of the tests is that they will indicate excessive leakage current which is responsible for RCDs tripping. Table 8.5 indicates maximum acceptable leakage currents for different types of appliance.

Some electronic equipment, such as computers and other data processors, normally have high earth leakage; this is because they are provided with filter circuits so that spikes and other mains disturbances are channelled to earth and do not damage them. Such equipment should not be connected by means of BS 12363 (13 A) sockets, but should be permanently connected or fed by BS 4343 industrial type sockets. Clearly, such equipment will give high earth leakage current, and this must be taken into account when assessing results.

8.4   TEST RECORDS
8.4.1   Why keep test records?
Much of the advantage of testing is lost if there is no system for recording which appliances have been tested, when the tests were carried out, and the results of these tests, as well as details of the methods of testing and the instruments used. The reasons for recording tests are two-fold:

1.   comparison of the present test results with those taken earlier will enable deterioration in performance to be seen at an early stage, so that the appliance concerned can be overhauled or discarded before it becomes dangerous, and

2.   being able to provide evidence of good test results will be important in the event of an accident.

It is imperative that there should be one responsible person in every organisation who knows that it is his duty to ensure that regular testing and recording of all portable appliances takes place.

8.4.2   What form should records take?

There is no stipulated form for the recording of portable appliance tests in the Electricity at Work Regulations, 1989. It would seem that the minimum sensible requirements would be:

1.   a log book or register of all the portable appliances in use at each establishment, together with details of how often each should be inspected and tested and where the appliance is normally to be found. To assist identification it would seem sensible to provide each appliance with its unique serial number, which can be written on a label affixed to it (*see* below). If a PAT with a bar code reader is used, and each appliance is bar coded, a scan will identify the appliance and will ensure that subsequent test results are ascribed to it. Perhaps it would be sensible to group appliances into categories, each requiring inspection and test at stipulated intervals. It should be the duty of a responsible person to inspect the book or register periodically to confirm that the required work is being carried out,

2.   a register of inspection and test results. As stated above, these will be required by a Health and Safety Inspector in the event of an accident or in the event of a routine or unsolicited inspection. The register provides essential information for the inspector and tester to enable deterioration of appliances to be spotted. A possible format for such a register appears below.

3.   a repair register. This should identify each piece of equipment repaired, the date on which the repair was carried out, full details of the nature of the work and full results of the tests carried out on the repaired item. Also

included should be the date on which the repaired appliance was put back into service,

4. a record of all faulty equipment. The list can be used to ensure that
    (a) faulty equipment is repaired and returned to service, or
    (b) unrepaired or irreparable equipment is not used.

APPLIANCE description ....

    location ....

    serial number ....

TESTS

Date due	Test date	Earth test (Ω)	Insul-ation ($M\Omega$)	Flash test (mA)	Pass/fail test P or F	Initials

5. a label for each appliance to indicate when the next inspection or test becomes due. Such a label could have the form shown below.

Serial number ....
TESTED AND PASSED
BY .... ON ....

NEXT TEST DUE ON ....
Any appliance which fails to meet the minimum standard must be immediately withdrawn from use. It will probably help to ensure that such equipment is not used if it is provided with a label such as that below:

Serial Number ....

EQUIPMENT NOT TO BE USED

REJECTED BY ....ON ....

REASON ....

Self adhesive labels with suitable wording are available from a number of suppliers.

Some test instruments have a built-in microprocessor which stores the test results and will print them out when connected to a suitable computer and printer. In this case, each appliance must be identified to the instrument, so it must be provided with a numeric or alphabetic keyboard to allow data input.

8.4.3   How often is it necessary to inspect and test?

There is no specified interval for inspection and test for portable appliances, and it is for each employer to set what is considered to be a safe interval. The period chosen may need to be defended in court after an accident, and should be based on:

1.   the type of appliance. For example, an electric drill which is used on a construction site is likely to need more frequent inspection and testing than a desk lamp,

2.   the usage of the equipment. A circular saw which is used only occasionally may need less frequent attention than an electric screwdriver which is in continuous use on a production line, and

3.   the manufacturer's recommendations. Most makers of portable appliances will suggest suitable periods for inspection and test schedules.

Suggested intervals between tests are shown in Table 8.1.

The Employer's Duties

9.1   ELECTRICAL SAFETY POLICY

There is no specific requirement for an electrical safety policy in the Electricity at Work Regulations 1989. However, these Regulations were drawn up as part of the Health and Safety at Work *etc*. Act, 1974, which does make a general statement on the subject. This reference is quoted below.

Health and Safety at Work *etc*. Act 1974
Section 2(3)
... it shall be the duty of every employer to prepare and .... revise a written statement of his general policy with respect to the health and safety at work of his employees and the organisation and arrangements .... for carrying out that policy ....

Whilst there is no specific mention of electrical safety, it must be remembered that the Act quoted above was enacted fifteen years before the Electricity at Work Regulations became law. It is therefore advisable that every employer, no matter how large or small, should produce a written statement of his policy regarding electrical safety.

9.2   STAFF COMPETENCE   (Regulation 16)

The Regulations require that all staff who use electricity in their work should be competent to deal with it, and that the systems and equipments that they use should have been designed and manufactured by those who are competent to do so. In a few cases all of the workers concerned will be direct employees, but usually the design and construction of electrical systems and equipments will have been carried out by others.

Because his workers will be using these systems and equipments, it is the responsibility of the employer to ensure that their design and construction is safe. When work is contracted out, for example when an electrical installation is installed or maintained by an electrical contractor, the employer must make sure that the work has been designed and carried out to provide a safe working environment for his employees. If the employer buys electrical equipment, such as electrically driven tools, he must make sure that they are safe for use.

In practice, a manufacturer of furniture, for example, is unlikely to be competent to assess the technical merit of an electrical contractor or of a supplier of electric tools. It is still his responsibility to do all he can to ensure that the electrical systems and devices he provides for the use of his workers are as safe as they can be. Where others are providing him with an expert service or a technical product, he has a right to expect that they will fulfil their obligations to him with competence.

Whether working directly for the employer, or indirectly by way of a contract or agreement to provide specialist goods or services, employees must be competent in respect of:

1. the specification of goods or services so that they will safely fulfil their requirements as far as is reasonably practicable,

2. the design of goods or services so that they can be expected to perform safely the duties required of them,

3. the erection and completion of electrical installations and other electrical works,

4. the completion of the work required directly for the employer,

5. the maintenance and testing of fixed electrical systems, and

6. the inspection and testing of portable appliances.

9.3   FIXED ELECTRICAL SYSTEMS

In most cases the employer will contract out work required for his electrical installation, although some employers do retain their own electrical installation staff. In the latter case it is probable that a specialist manager will be employed to oversee the operations of the electrical installation staff.

In either case, the employer must be sure that those responsible for the work are competent in terms of:

1.   a proper assessment of the requirements so that full information is available to the designer of the system concerned,

2.   correct and expert design of the system so that it will meet the needs of its users in terms of safety and efficiency,

3.   the proper specification of switchgear, protective devices, cables, and so on,

4.   the safe and efficient installation of the complete system,

5.   the inspection and testing of the completed installation to ensure that it has been correctly and safely installed,

6.   correct commissioning of the installation to confirm that the designers and specifiers have correctly foreseen the requirements of the users, and

7.   the provision of full and detailed information concerning the installation as required by the IEE Wiring Regulations   (BS 7671).

9.4   PORTABLE TOOLS AND EQUIPMENT (Regulation 10)

In this respect, the employer is responsible first for selecting and specifying the proper appliances so that his workers can safely complete the tasks they are set. Secondly, he is responsible for ensuring that a proper system is put in place for the inspection and testing of all portable equipments at the correct intervals in terms of the uses to which they are put.

He must also ensure that a system of recording for the test results is maintained and is available to the test and inspection personnel. Finally, he must ensure that the proper equipment is available to carry out testing on portable equipment (*see* Chapter 8). This may be the property of his own organisation, or may belong to a competent contractor who is employed for the purpose of testing.

9.5   MAINTAINING PROPER RECORDS

The employer must keep records which enable him to show that he has complied with the spirit of the Electricity at Work Regulations 1989. These records will comprise the following:

1.   design data for the electrical installations used in his establishment, to include calculations relevant to the proper selection of equipment. Such data will be required by those who carry out the periodic inspections and tests of the installation, and may also be required by Health and Safety Inspectors in the event of routine inspection or of an accident,

2.   specifications relating to the original electrical installation,

3.   "as fitted" drawings, details of the mains and submains layout, and all other relevant information required by the IEE Wiring Regulations (BS 7671),

4.   a schedule of the proposed and the actual dates for re-testing and inspection of the installation, together with the results of all such work already completed,

5.   the schedule of portable appliances in use at the premises, together with details of the programme of periodic inspection and testing, with the tabulated results of such tests,

6.   details of the expertise and competence of all personnel employed, including dated qualifications, information concerning specialist training and education courses, and so on.

Items 1 to 4 may well form part of the Electrical Installation Operational Manual, provision of which is now a requirement of the *Requirements for Electrical Installations, BS 7671*, commonly known as the 16th Edition of the IEE Wiring Regulations.

Appendix 1
The Electricity at Work Regulations 1989

Made - - - -	7th April 1989
Laid before Parliament - -	25th April 1989
Coming into force - - -	1st April 1990

PART I GENERAL

Citation and comment

1.   These Regulations may be cited as the Electricity at Work Regulations 1989 and shall come into force on 1st April 1990.

Interpretation

2.   (1)   In these Regulations, unless the context otherwise requires:

"approved" means approved in writing at the time being by the Health and Safety Executive for the purposes of these Regulations or conforming with a specification approved in writing by the Health and Safety Executive for the purposes of these Regulations;

"circuit conductor" means any conductor in a system which is intended to carry electric current in normal conditions, or to be energised in normal conditions, and includes a combined neutral and earth conductor, but does not include a conductor provided solely to perform a protective function by connection to earth or other reference point;

"conductor" means a conductor of electrical energy;

"danger" means risk of injury;

"electrical equipment" includes anything used, intended to be used or installed for use, to generate, provide, transmit, transform, rectify, convert, conduct, distribute, control, store, measure or use electrical energy;

"firedamp" means any flammable gas or any flammable mixture of gases occurring naturally in a mine;

"injury" means death or personal injury from electric shock, electric burn, electrical explosion or arcing, or from fire or explosion initiated by electrical energy, where any such death or injury is associated with the generation, provision, transmission, transformation, rectification, conversion, conduction, distribution, control, storage, measurement or use of electrical energy;

"safety-lamp mine" means —
   (a)   any coal mine; or
   (b)   any other mine in which —
          (i)   there has occurred below ground an ignition of firedamp; or
          (ii)   more than 0.25% by volume of firedamp is found on any occasion at any place below ground in the mine;

"system" means an electrical system in which all the electrical equipment is, or may be, electrically connected to a common source of electrical energy, which includes such source and such equipment.

(2)   Unless the context otherwise requires, any reference in these Regulations to —
   (a)   a numbered regulation or Schedule is a reference to the regulation or Schedule in these Regulations so numbered;
   (b)   a numbered paragraph is a reference to the paragraph so numbered in the regulation or Schedule in which the reference appears.

Persons on whom duties are imposed by these Regulations

3.   (1) Except where otherwise expressly provided in these Regulations, it shall be the duty of every-
   (a) employer and self-employed person to comply with the provisions of these Regulations in so far as they relate to matters which are within his control; and

(b) manager of a mine or quarry (within in either case the meaning of section 180 of the Mines and Quarries Act 1954(a)) to ensure that all requirements or prohibitions imposed by or under these Regulations are complied with in so far as they relate to the mine or quarry or part of a quarry of which he is the manager and to matters which are within his control.

(2) It shall be the duty of every employee while at work-

(a) to co-operate with his employer so far as is necessary to enable any duty placed on that employer by the provisions of these Regulations to be complied with; and

(b)   to comply with the provisions of these Regulations in so far as they relate to matters which are within his control.

PART II GENERAL
Systems, work activities and protective equipment

4.   (1)   All systems shall at all times be of such construction as to prevent, so far as is reasonably practicable, danger.

(2)   As may be necessary to prevent danger, all systems shall be maintained so as to prevent, so far as is reasonably practicable, such danger.

(3)   Every work activity, including operation, use and maintenance of a system and work near a system, shall be carried out in such a manner as not to give rise, so far as is reasonably practicable, to danger.

(4)   Any equipment provided under these Regulations for the purpose of protecting persons at work on or near electrical equipment shall be suitable for the use for which it is provided, be maintained in a condition suitable for that use, and be properly used.

Strength and capability of electrical equipment

5.   No electrical equipment shall be put into use where its strength and capability may be exceeded in such a way as may give rise to danger.

Adverse or hazardous environments

6.   Electrical equipment which may be reasonably forseeably exposed
to —

    (a)   mechanical damage;

    (b)   the effects of the weather, natural hazards, tempera
ture or pressure;

    (c)   the effects of wet, dirty, dusty or corrosive conditions;   or

    (d)   any flammable or explosive substance, including dusts,
vapours or gases, shall be of such construction or as
necessary protected as to prevent, so far as is reason
ably practicable, danger arising from such exposure.

Insulation, protection and placing of conductors

7.   All conductors in a system which may give rise to danger shall either

    (a)   be suitably covered with insulating material and as necessary
protected so as to prevent, so far as is reasonably practicable, danger; or

    (b)   have such precautions taken in respect of them (including,
where appropriate, their being suitably placed) as will prevent, so far as is
reasonably practicable, danger.

Earthing or other suitable precautions

8.   Precautions shall be taken, either by earthing or by other suitable
means, to prevent danger arising when any conductor (other than a circuit
conductor) which may reasonably forseeably become charged as a result of
either the use of the system, or a fault in a system, becomes so charged; and,
for the purposes of ensuring compliance with this regulation, a conductor
shall be regarded as earthed when it is connected to the general mass of
earth by conductors of sufficient strength and current-carrying capability to
discharge electrical energy to earth.

Integrity of referenced conductors

9.   If a circuit conductor is connected to earth or to any other reference
point, nothing which might reasonably be expected to give rise to danger by
breaking the electrical continuity or introducing high impedance shall be

placed in that conductor unless suitable precautions are taken to prevent that danger.

Connections

10.   Where necessary to prevent danger, every joint and connection in a system shall be mechanically and electrically suitable for use.

Means for protecting from excess of current

11.   Efficient means, suitably located, shall be provided for protecting from excess of current every part of a system as may be necessary to prevent danger.

Means for cutting off the supply and for isolation

12.   (1) Subject to paragraph (3), where necessary to prevent danger, suitable means, (including, where appropriate, methods of identifying circuits) shall be available for —

    (a)   cutting off the supply of electrical energy to any electrical equipment; and

    (b)   the isolation of any electrical equipment.

    (2) In paragraph (1), "isolation" means the disconnection and separation of the electrical equipment from every source of electrical energy in such a way that this disconnection and separation is secure.

    (3)   Paragraph (1) shall not apply to electrical equipment which is itself a source of electrical energy but, in such a case as is necessary, precautions shall be taken to prevent, so far as is reasonably practicable, danger.

Precautions for work on equipment made dead

13.   Adequate precautions shall be taken to prevent electrical equipment, which has been made dead in order to prevent danger while work is carried out on or near that equipment, from becoming electrically charged during that work if danger may thereby arise.

Work on or near live conductors

14.   No person shall be engaged in any work activity on or so near any live conductor (other than one suitably covered with insulating material so as to prevent danger) that danger may arise unless —

      (a)   it is unreasonable in all the circumstances for it to be dead; and

      (b)   it is reasonable in all the circumstances for him to be at work on or near it while it is live; and

      (c)   suitable precautions (including where necessary the provision of suitable protective equipment) are taken to prevent injury.

Working space, access and lighting

15.   For the purposes of enabling injury to be prevented, adequate working space, adequate means of access, and adequate lighting shall be provided at all electrical equipment on which or near which work is being done in circumstances which may give rise to danger.

Persons to be competent to prevent danger and injury

16.   No person shall be engaged in any work activity where technical knowledge or experience is necessary to prevent danger or, where appropriate, injury, unless he possesses such knowledge or experience, or is under such degree of supervision as may be appropriate having regard to the nature of the work.

PART III REGULATIONS APPLYING TO MINES ONLY

Regulations 17 to 28 inclusive are omitted here because this Guide is not concerned with them.

PART IV MISCELLANEOUS AND GENERAL
Defence

29.   In any proceedings for an offence consisting of a contravention of regulations 4(4), 5, 8, 9, 10, 11, 12, 13, 14, 15, 16, or 25, it shall be a defence

for any person to prove that he took all reasonable steps and exercised all due diligence to avoid the commission of that offence.

Exemption certificates

30.   (1)   subject to paragraph (2), the Health and Safety Executive may, by a certificate in writing, exempt —

      (a)   any person;
      (b)   any premises;
      (c)   any electrical equipment;
      (d)   any electrical system;
      (e)   any electrical process;
      (f)   any activity,

or any class of the above, from any requirement or prohibition imposed by these Regulations and any such exemption may be granted subject to conditions and to a limit of time and may be revoked by a certificate in writing at any time.

(2)   The Executive shall not grant any such exemption unless, having regard to the circumstances of the case, and in particular to —

      (a)   the conditions, if any, which it proposes to attach to the exemption; and

      (b)   any other requirements imposed by or under any enactment which apply to the case, it is satisfied that the health and safety of persons who are likely to be affected by the exemption will not be prejudiced in consequence of it.

Extension outside Great Britain

31.   These Regulations shall apply to and in relation to premises and activities outside Great Britain to which sections 1 to 59 and 80 to 82 of the Health and Safety at Work etc. Act 1974 apply by virtue of articles 6 and 7 of the Health and Safety at Work etc. Act 1974 (Application outside Great Britain) Order 1977(a) as they apply within Great Britain.

Disapplication of duties

32.   The duties imposed by these Regulations shall not extend to-

        (a)   the master or crew of a sea-going ship or to the employer of such persons, in relation to the normal ship-board activities of a ship's crew under the direction of the master; or

        (b)   any person, in relation to any aircraft or hovercraft which is moving under its own power.

Revocations and modifications

33.   (1)   The instruments specified in column 1 of Part I of Schedule 2 are revoked to the extent specified in the corresponding entry in column 3 of that part.

        (2)   The enactments and instruments specified in Part II of Schedule 2 shall be modified to the extent specified in that Part.

        (3)   In the Mines and Quarries Act 1954, the Mines and Quarries (Tips) Act 1969(b) and the Mines Management Act 1971(c), and in regulations made under any of those Acts, or in health and safety regulations, any reference to any of those Acts shall be treated as including a reference to these Regulations.

Signed by order of the Secretary of State

                                                        Patrick Nicholls

Parliamentary Under Secretary of State,

Department of Employment

7th April 1989

Alphabetical Index to the Regulations

The numbers shown refer to the paragraphs in the Regulations which are reproduced in the first part off this Appendix

Appendix 2
Publications

Safety Publications of the Health and Safety Executive and the Health and Safety Commission

Ref	Title	Relevant Regs
GS 6	Avoidance of danger from overhead electric lines	4, 14, 15, 16
GS 23	Electrical safety in schools	4, 6, 7, 8, 10, 11, 12, 14, 16.
GS 24	Electricity on construction sites	4 to 16
GS 27	Protection against electric shock	4, 6, 7, 8.
GS 33	Avoiding danger from buried electric cables	4, 14, 16.
GS 34	Electrical safety in departments of electrical engineering	4, 6, 7, 8, 12, 13, 14, 15, 16.
GS 37	Flexible leads, plugs, sockets etc	5, 6, 7, 8, 10, 11.
GS 38	Electrical test equipment for use by electricians	5, 6, 7, 10, 14, 16.
GS 44	Electrical working practices	4, 7, 12, 13, 14, 15, 16.
PM 29	Electrical hazards from steam/water pressure cleaners	4, 6, 7, 8, 10.
PM 32	The safe use of portable electrical apparatus	4, 6, 7, 8, 9, 10, 11, 12.
PM37	Electrical installations in motor vehicle repair premises	4, 5, 6, 7, 8, 10, 11, 12,16.
PM 38	Selection and use of electric handlamps	4, 6, 7, 8, 10, 12.
PM 51	Safety in the use of radio frequency dielectric heating equipment	4, 7, 8, 12, 13, 16.

PM 53	Emergency private generation: electrical safety	4, 5, 6, 7, 8, 9, 10, 11, 12
PM 64	Electrical safety in arc welding	4, 6, 7, 8, 10, 12, 14, 16.
OP 10	Safety of electrical distribution systems on factory premises	4, 5, 7, 8, 9, 10, 13, 16
HS(G)13	Electrical testing	4, 7, 12, 13, 14, 15, 16.
HS(G)22	Electrical apparatus for use in potentially explosive atmospheres	4, 5, 6.
HS(G)38	Lighting at work	4, 13, 14, 15

H S C and Foundry Industry Advisory Committee
publication ISBN 0 11 883909 8

| Safe use of electric induction furnaces | 4, 5, 6, 7, 8,14, 15, 16. |

British Standards and Codes of Practice

Ref	Title	Relevant Regs
BS 162	Specification for electric power switchgear (partly replaced by BS 5486 and BS 5227)	4, 5, 12, 15
BS697	Specification for rubber gloves for electrical purposes	4, 14
BS 921	Rubber mats for electrical purposes	4, 14
BS CP 1003	Electrical apparatus for use in explosive atmospheres of gas or vapour other than mining applications	4, 6
BS CP 1013	Earthing	8
BS CP 1017	Distribution of electricity on construction and building sites	4, 6, 10
BS CP 1101	Maintenance of electric motor control gear	4
BS 2754	Construction of electrical equipment for protection against electric shock.	7, 8
BS 2771	Electrical equipment of industrial	4, 6

	machines(partly replaced by BS 6423 and BS 6626)	
BS 3456	Household electrical appliances	5
BS 4363	Specification for distribution units for electricity supplies for construction and building sites	4, 6, 10
BS 4444	Guide to electrical earth monitoring	8
BS 4533	Safety of luminaires	5
BS 4999	General requirements for rotating electrical machines. Classification of types of enclosure	6, 7
BS 5253	Specification for AC disconnectors (isolators) and earthing switches.	12
BS 5419	Specification for air-break switches, air-break disconnectors and fuse combination units	12
BS 5435	Code of practice for selection, installation and maintenance of electrical apparatus for use in potentially explosive atmospheres (other than mining applications or explosive processing and manufacture)	4, 6
BS 5405	Code of practice for the maintenance of electrical switchgear (partly replaced by BS 6423 and BS 6626)	4, 13, 16
BS 5420	Specification for degrees of protection of enclosures of switchgear and control gear	6, 7
BS 5490	Specification for classification of degrees of protection provided by enclosures	6, 7
BS 5501	Electrical equipment for potentially explosive atmospheres	4, 6
BS 5655	Safety rules for the construction and operation of electric lifts.	15

BS 5784	Safety of electrical commercial catering equipoment	5
BS 5958	Code of practice for control of undesirable static electricity	6
BS 6423	Code of practice for maintenance of electrical switchgear and control gear	4, 12, 13
BS 6467	Electrical apparatus with protection by enclosure for use in the presence of combustible dusts.	6
BS PD 6519	Effects of current passing through the human body	2
BS 6626	Code of practice for maintenance of electrical switchgear and control gear	4, 12, 13
BS 6651	Code of practice for protection of structures against lightning	6
BS 6742	Electrostatic painting and finishing equipment using flammable materials	6
BS 7671	Regulations for electrical installations	All

Publications of the Institution of Electrical Engineers

Regulations for Electrical Installations (16th Edition) commonly known as the IEE Wiring Regulations) and published as BS 7671.
Associated Guidance notes published as;

The On-Site Guide	
Guidance Note 1	Selection and erection
Guidance Note 2	Isolation and switching
Guidance Note 3	Inspection and testing
Guidance Note 4	Protection against fire
Guidance Note 5	Protection against electric shock
Guidance Note 6	Protection against overcurrent
Guidance Note 7	Special installations and locations

Alphabetical Index to Publications

Appendix 3
Cross-Reference Index

Regulation number	Guide reference
Regulation 1	Introduction
Regulation 2	1.2, 2.1, 2.2, 3.1, 6.1.
Regulation 3	1.2.1, 1.3, 1.4, 3.2, 3.3, 7.1.1, 7.1.2.
Regulation 4	6.5, 7.2, 7.3, 8.2, 8.3.
Regulation 5	1.4.1, 4.2, 4.3, 4.4, 4.5.
Regulation 6	1.3, 1.4.2, 4.2, 4.6.
Regulation 7	1.3, 1.4.2, 6.6.
Regulation 8	1.4.1, 6.7.
Regulation 9	1.4.1, 6.8.1.
Regulation 10	1.4.1, 4.7, 6.8.2, 8.2, 8.3, 9.4.
Regulation 11	1.4.1, 4.8.
Regulation 12	1.4.1, 4.9, 7.4.
Regulation 13	1.4.1, 7.5.1.
Regulation 14	1.2.1, 1.3, 1.4.1, 7.5.2, 7.6.
Regulation 15	1.3, 1.4.1, 5.2, 5.3.
Regulation 16	1.2.1, 1.4.1, 2.1, 3.1, 3.2, 3.3, 9.2.
Regulations 17 to 28	apply to mines and quarries only.
Regulation 29	1.4
Regulation 30	1.5.1.
Regulation 31	1.5.2.
Regulation 32	1.5.3.
Regulation 33	1.5.4.

Alphabetical Index